AN HERBAL
FEAST

AN HERBAL FEAST

HERBALISTS
SHARE
THEIR
FAVORITE
RECIPES

Risa Mornis

Illustrations by Adrienne Metcalfe

Keats Publishing, Inc.   New Canaan, Connecticut

An Herbal Feast is not intended as medical advice. Its intent is solely infor-mational and educational. Please consult a health professional should the need for one be indicated.

AN HERBAL FEAST
Copyright © 1998 by Risa Mornis
All Rights Reserved

Library of Congress Cataloging-in-Publication Data

Mornis, Rita.
    An herbal feast : herbalists share their favorite recipes / Risa
Mornis : illustrated by Adrienne Metcalfe.
        p.   cm.
    Includes bibliographical references and index.
    ISBN 0-87983-801-9
    1. Cookery (Herbs)   2. Herbs.   I. Title.
TX819.H4M68   1998
641.6'57—dc21   98-11633
                                                              CIP

Printed in the United States of America
ISBN: 0-87983-801-9

Keats Publishing, Inc.
27 Pine Street (Box 876)
New Canaan, Connecticut 06840-0876
Website address: www.keats.com

To my husband Jeff,
for his love, understanding and patience
and for my children,
Avery and Sara,
with love

CONTENTS

Acknowledgments   ix

Introduction   1

Harvesting Your Own Herbs   3

Appetizers & Salads   6

Snacks   21

Beverages   24

Dips, Sandwiches & Spreads   46

Vinegars & Dressings   62

Soups   75

Sauces   94

Breads & Butters   103

Vegetables   119

Main Dishes   130

Desserts   175

Breakfast Dishes   197

Appendix of Healing Herbs   205

Herbalists' Profiles   211

Recommended Reading   251

Index   253

ACKNOWLEDGMENTS

So many people helped this book come into existence. The contributors are the champions of this book and deserve special thanks for believing in it and being the source of my inspiration. There are so many wonderful herbalists out there doing great work, and this book is for and by them.

I could not have survived the last three-week stretch working on this book without the loving care of my inlaws, Vivian and Joe Mornis. Thank you, Viv and Joe, for watching and caring for my children (plus my husband and me) during that stressful time. Special thanks also goes to Lisa Kaija and Debbie Hammett and their children for keeping my children busy and happy. The manuscript would still be in the computer if not for these master babysitters. Thanks go to the playgroup moms, Jane Smolnik and her apprenticeship class, Julie Manchester, Tracy Wilkinson and Martha Mott for cooking and tasting. Special thanks to my editor, Phyllis Herman, for making this all possible and to my illustrator, Adrienne, for adding the beautiful drawings.

Thank you Kim for coming to visit three weeks before my deadline and making me take a break. Thank you, Steve, Marie, Daniel and Teresa, for coming to visit the week before my deadline. Your vacation energy lightened me up and kept me going to the end. And to you too, Bryn, for coming after it was all finished and helping me celebrate. Thanks to my sister and her husband, Lori and Peter Weston, for encouraging me in my writing path—and suggesting the newsletter that eventually led me to this book. Thanks also to my brothers, Joel, Nam and Jose, for your love and humor. Thanks to Grandmom Julia for encouraging me in my "natural" path. And to you too, Joy, for your constant interest and encouragement. And to Grandmother and Granddad for your kind hearts and loving presence. For you, Mom and Dad, go hugs and kisses for being who you are and helping me be who I am. My children, Avery and Sara, were both my motivation and my distraction. They kept me balanced and sane.

The most thanks of all go to my husband Jeff, the love of my life, for enduring the light on in the office/bedroom until 12 a.m. for two weeks in a row, cleaning the house, killing the ants, eating cereal for dinner, watering the wilting house plants, chopping the wood, clearing the driveway, mowing the lawn, feeding the chickens, taking out the trash, not to mention working for a living, plus all the other things you did without me noticing. I love you.

A final special thank you to the dream fairy who was flitting around in my head that night I was reading cookbooks and gave me the idea for this book.

INTRODUCTION

Before the idea for this book came about, I wanted to learn how to incorporate more herbs into my family's diet, but my knowledge of the edible and nutritional value of herbs was not as strong as my medicinal knowledge. I started out trying recipes by other herbalists and naturalists to boost my confidence. With more experience came the knowledge that there were others like me looking for good herbal food recipes. Since I began compiling this book, I have come to know more and more herbalists, enjoyed a wide range of recipes, expanded my family's experience with different tastes and have felt a positive change in our health and energy levels. With the greater presence of greens in our diet has come a stronger respect for the earth and its ability to provide for us.

Herbs have been used in food for so long that we take them for granted. They sit on our shelves or over our stoves for years and years and we forget we have them. When we remember, we put a dash of lifeless, tasteless supermarket herb on our food hoping it will taste a little more interesting. This book is not about these ancient dried-out herbs; it is about fresh garden herbs, wild herbs and those dried herbs that are less than a year old. On the other hand, this is not a gourmet cookbook. It is a "take what you have and use it" book. These recipes come from people who do not necessarily cook for a living, but do cook to live. You will find both the simple and the complex, recipes for both beginner and advanced cooks—but they all reflect life in the kitchen of an herbalist. Some of us prefer garden herbs, others prefer the wild ones. In this book you'll find both.

An important component of this book is the information about each herbalist. We each have our own individual focus and special interests, but we do have a common ground: a fascination with plants and their usefulness to humankind. The herbalists profiled here are valued in their communities for their work with and for plants, and each one represents at least 30 more who did not make it into the book. There are thousands of herbalists all over the world, an uncounted number that has slowly decreased in the last century. However, the resurgence of interest in herbs has helped to slow that decrease and turn it around. Despite this growth in interest, herbs are still not used to their full capacity. The purpose of this book is to help you include wild and garden herbs in your diet. Who could better teach you than herbalists themselves! We, who are in constant connection with the properties of herbs—edible, medicinal, and aesthetic—are delighted to share the recipes that have brought us closer to plants, the earth and an understanding of ourselves.

HOW TO USE THIS BOOK

Each recipe is accompanied by the name of the herbalist or organization that contributed it at the bottom. Turn to the Herbalists' Profiles beginning on page 211 for a brief biography of each that includes an address, phone number (in most cases) and in some cases an e-mail and/or Website page address.

FRESH OR DRIED HERBS?

Unless otherwise indicated the herbs in the recipes are dried herbs. Fresh can be substituted in most of the recipes. Generally speaking, one part dried herb equals three parts fresh. For one teaspoon of dried marjoram, substitute three teaspoons fresh marjoram. If you are like the majority of herbalists and do not like to measure, one handful of fresh uncut herb is roughly equivalent to one teaspoon of dry herb. However, this is not the case for seeds. Fresh or dried, their measurement is the same.

HARVESTING YOUR OWN HERBS

There are many good books available to help determine a plant's best harvesting time (See a list of my favorite herbals on page 251). For strongest flavor, the best time to harvest herbs for drying is either before or as they flower. If you want to use the fresh herb, you can harvest at any time. Herbs will grow much better if pruned regularly. Use sharp, clean scissors and pick a warm, sunny morning before the sun is too strong, but after the dew has evaporated from the plants. Always pick the youngest, greenest, best-looking parts of the plant and dust and shake them clean of any dirt, debris or bugs. If you are using the plant fresh, wash it well before using. If you are drying it for future use, shake and wipe it clean as best you can before hanging it or laying it flat to dry. Do not wash it. The plant may mildew or rot before it manages to dry.

Many of the herbs used in these recipes are "weeds" growing between cultivated herbs. Dandelion, purslane, chickweed and lamb's quarters are edible and medicinal weeds that grow in every garden. Don't forget to pick and enjoy them as you are harvesting your other herbs.

WILDCRAFTING

Harvesting plants from the wild is a tradition and an act of reverence that has brought great understanding to the living patterns of plants and their many uses. The current fear among herbalists, though, is the fear of plant extinction. There are many plants in danger of becoming extinct because of overharvesting and a disregard for, or ignorance of the fragility of plant environments.

What can you do to help? When harvesting, do so with the plants' best interests in mind. First, be sure it is not on your area's endangered plant list. Next, notice how many plants are growing in the spot you are harvesting. Only two or three plants? Don't harvest. A family of six or more? Harvest one-third or less. It is important to insure the survival of the plants you harvest for your own future use as well as for the welfare of the planet. Planting seeds of the plant can also help insure its survival.

Do not harvest a plant if you are unsure of its identity. Take along an identification book (and/or an herbalist) to confirm its identity before assuming what it is. Always ask your neighbors before harvesting on their land and do not harvest under power lines or near well-traveled roads. Plants exposed to heavy traffic absorb pollutants from automobiles. Be sure that the field or yard that you harvest in has not been sprayed with chemical fertilizers. Optimum nutrition and medicine do not come from chemically laden plants. If you are harvesting a lot of one plant, consider growing it in your own garden or yard for your benefit as well as for the plants' survival.

Last, but most important, remember that you are taking a living plant. Respect your partnership with it and request its permission before harvesting. Give it something in return: plant its seeds, give it a beautiful stone, add some compost or manure.

More and more people are learning about and using wild plants for food and medicine. Because of this, plant environments are becoming more stressed. Be aware of your potentially negative impact on plants and harvest with care and respect for the future.

Fresh Herbs

The best way to use herbs is fresh. Herbs do not have to be dried before being used. Drying is important for using herbs during the winter, but not essential for consumption. The taste of fresh herbs in food can not be surpassed, and their health benefits are tripled. Every day go out and pick a few fresh herbs for your omelet, sandwich, salad or meal. As you become more familiar with herbs and wild edible weeds, you won't be able to resist the urge to pick them, wash them and add them to your lunch.

DRYING HERBS

The quicker you dry your herbs, the better the color and flavor will be. However, do not dry them in direct sunlight or at high temperatures as this destroys the properties of the plants. An oven set at its lowest temperature with the door open or an airy dust-free area will do the trick. You can make an herb-drying rack out of a clothes rack; hang herbs from beams, hangers or other contraptions; or lay small herb pieces out on screens, paper plates or newspapers. The choices are endless. Use your creativity and work with your space.

Leaves and flowers can be hung by their stems. The material is dry when it is just becoming crisp. Wash, dry and chop roots up while still fresh. Lay them out on trays, screens or newspapers. They can be dried in the sun as long as the light is indirect, in the oven or just in a warm place. They are dry when they snap or feel lighter. This could take a month or longer. For seeds, cut the whole seed head as it is turning from green to brown. Separate from insects and place in a cloth bag. Hang to dry. Leave for one to two months or until crunchy.

APPETIZERS & SALADS

LAMB'S QUARTERS/TOMATO/ CUCUMBER SALAD

⅓ onion
1 medium cucumber
1 medium tomato
Several large handfuls of lamb's
   quarters
Wild oregano to taste

Salt, pepper, chives, Spike to
   taste
Sprig of parsley
Oil and vinegar to taste
Borage flowers

Toss first seven ingredients with oil and vinegar and garnish with the borage flowers. Serves 2.

—FEATHER JONES, ROCKY MOUNTAIN CENTER FOR BOTANICAL STUDIES

"GOOD MEDICINE" SALAD

Who says that medicine has to taste bad? This colorful salad is full of vitamins and minerals and the health-giving qualities of fresh garlic, wild greens, organic veggies and fresh herbs.

2 cups cooked brown rice (can be part millet or another grain)
¼ cup cold-pressed, extra virgin olive oil
1 large cucumber, grated
2 cups wild greens: chickweed, lamb's quarters, dandelion, amaranth in any combination
½ cup dulse seaweed, chopped
½ cup almonds, chopped
¼ cup sesame seeds
2–4 large cloves garlic, minced
¼ cup diced red pepper or raw beet, grated
¼ cup fresh parsley, chopped
2 Tbsp. fresh tarragon, chopped
2 Tbsp. fresh dill, chopped
Tamari or shoyu soy sauce

Combine all the ingredients except the tamari or soy sauce in a large bowl and mix thoroughly. Add a little tamari or soy sauce to taste. Serve at room temperature over a bed of lettuce. You can also substitute small amounts of the following: red or white cabbage, carrots, celery, umeboshi or brown rice vinegar. Serves 4–6

—BARBARA NARDOZZI

TOMATO HERB SALAD

3 very ripe tomatoes with the skins removed (Immerse in boiling water for 12 seconds and the skins will easily slip off.)
2 sprigs fresh basil
1 sprig fresh lemon thyme
1 sprig fresh fennel
2 cloves garlic
Olive oil, to taste

Chop up tomatoes, herbs and garlic. Mix together with olive oil and refrigerate for an hour before eating. Serves 4–6.

—ANDREA ROGERS, VINEYARD VINES

Calendula

Pot marigold (*Calendula officinalis*) has long been appreciated for its beauty in the garden. One of its modern uses is in salves as an astringent, anti-inflammatory and antifungal ingredient. Less well known is its use as a substitute for saffron. To dry your own garden calendula, pull the petals apart and arrange them without touching each other on a large cookie sheet. If they overlap, the result will be blackening or loss of color. Dry in an oven that has been heated to 200° F and then turned off. When crisp, store in a glass, ceramic or stoneware jar in a cool, dark place. Add to soups, stews and rice. (This is *not* the same plant as the African marigold. Be sure the Latin name of your plant is *Calendula officinalis.*)

"THE DEVIL MADE ME DO IT" EGGS

Start one dozen eggs in cold water with ½ Tbs. salt added. Bring slowly to a rolling boil. Cover and simmer for 20 minutes. Drain and cool. Peel off shells and cut eggs in half. Remove yolk. To the yolk, add to taste:

Mayonnaise
Fresh onion, finely chopped
Calendula flower petals
Blue borage flowers
Fresh dill

Fresh garlic, finely chopped
Parsley (optional)
Nasturtium, pansy, carnation or
   rose petals for garnish

Fill egg whites with the yolk mixture and decorate with nasturtium, pansy, carnation or rose petals. Keep chilled before serving. Serves 10–12.

—FEATHER JONES, ROCKY MOUNTAIN CENTER FOR BOTANICAL STUDIES

TOMATO, BASIL AND RED ONION SALAD

5 large ripe tomatoes
2 large red onions, sliced
⅓ cup tarragon vinegar

¼ cup extra virgin olive oil
Salt and pepper to taste
20 leaves of fresh basil

Slice the tomatoes ½-inch thick; slice the onions thinly. Arrange alternating slices of tomato and onion on a serving platter. Drizzle tarragon vinegar and olive oil over salad. Sprinkle the salad with salt and pepper to taste and garnish with basil leaves. Serves 10.

—JUDITH GRAVES, LAMBS & THYME

SUSHI SALAD

2 cups cooked rice	*Dressing:*
1 avocado	¼ cup water
6 straw mushrooms	¼ cup apple cider vinegar
1 cup prepared crabmeat	⅛ cup soy sauce
1 cup cucumber	½ tsp. wasabi horseradish
¼ cup wakami seaweed	1 Tbsp. sugar
½ sweet red (or green) pepper	1 tsp. powdered ginger
2 cloves wild garlic	1 Tbsp. sesame seeds
4 wild scallions (entire)	1 tsp. poppy seeds
1 root of wild ginger (optional)	½ tsp. dried rosemary
	½ tsp. dried marjoram

Cut all salad ingredients into bitesize (or smaller) pieces, and place in a bowl. Combine dressing ingredients in a pan, stirring over low heat until mixture is smooth. Pour dressing over salad and refrigerate in a covered dish for at least an hour to blend flavors. Makes a festive red and green dish that is best enjoyed the same day to retain color and crispness. Serves 6–8.

—Sheryl Allyn, Wilderness Way School

SPICY KELP RINGS

2 cups peeled, sliced kelp (*Nereocystis luetkeana*)
1 cup salsa, medium or hot

Marinate kelp rings in salsa for 24–48 hours, stirring occasionally. Remove from marinade and dry kelp in vegetable dehydrator (or an oven with a pilot light). Store in a glass jar. These spicy chewy rings are super as a snack or appetizer. Makes 2 cups.

—Janice Schofield

Seaweeds

Seaweeds are eaten by coastal people around the world. Their high vitamin and mineral content provide excellent nourishment for the body. Studies have shown that kelp seaweeds (*phaephyceae*) protect the body from radioactive and environmental contaminants, ever-increasing threats to the health of humans and all life on earth. Japanese research has shown them to be beneficial for lowering blood pressure and cholesterol levels. Kelp is thought to help heal gastric and duodenal ulcers and colitis. Daily use of seaweeds helps boost stamina and offset stress.

There are many types of edible seaweeds to choose from. If you are unfamiliar with the taste of seaweed, start with mild-tasting hijiki or arame. There is more calcium in one tablespoon of hijiki than in an 8-ounce glass of milk.

BAKED GARLIC

Clean one whole head of garlic of its loose outer leaves and clip off the top of it. Rub with olive oil. Put in a baking dish with water up to ½ of the head. Add herb sprigs (oregano, thyme, rosemary, basil) to the water. Bake at 350° F for about 1 hour. Squeeze out on bread or crackers while warm. Usually about ½ head per person will suffice, except for true garlic lovers, who will devour a whole head or more easily! The biggest problem is people who are shy about squeezing the cloves. Go for it!

—CASCADE ANDERSON GELLER

Harvesting Mushrooms

Seek out your local naturalist for knowledge of wild mushrooms before harvesting and eating them. Never taste a mushroom to determine edibility. Just a tiny bite of *Amanita virosa* can kill a child. Death by mushroom poisoning is slow and painful. When learning by book, only use guides written in and for the country in which you are harvesting. The more regional guides are the better choices. Always cross-reference between two or more guides before using any mushroom. If there is any doubt of identity, do not use the mushroom. Mushrooming can be a deadly hobby. Read the introductions, instructions and cautions in guides before embarking on this adventure!

WILD MUSHROOM CAVIAR

As with caviar, this dish may be too salty for some tastes. I often reduce the salt by half to let the mushroom flavor dominate.

¼ cup butter
½ cup finely chopped wild leeks
⅛ tsp. salt
¼ tsp. pepper
½ tsp. tamari
⅛ tsp. honey

1 cup chopped mushrooms (Morels, oyster, inky caps, beefsteaks, chanterelle and shaggy manes are good for beginning foragers, but be careful!)

Sauté the leeks in butter to soften. Add the rest of the ingredients and stir to mix well. Cook over medium heat for 10–15 minutes, or until all the liquid has evaporated. Adjust seasonings when mixture has finished cooking. Allow to cool. Use this mixture as a topping for breads or as a filling for pastas, fish or meat roulades. Makes about 1 cup.

—JOYCE WARDWELL

PICKLED GINGER

Ginger works wonderfully in aiding digestion. It is also good for the nausea associated with traveling and for morning sickness. This delicious recipe is great since you can take it anywhere.

8 oz. fresh ginger
Sea salt
1 Tbsp. sugar
1 cup rice vinegar

Peel the ginger, and slice as thinly as possible. Place the slices in a non-metallic bowl and cover with cold water. Let sit for ½ hour. Drain the ginger, put in a pot of boiling water, return to the boil, drain and let cool. Return ginger to the bowl and sprinkle with salt. Add the sugar and vinegar to the pot. Simmer over low heat and stir until the sugar has dissolved. Pour the vinegar mixture over the ginger, completely submerging it. Cover the bowl and let sit for 3 weeks in a cool dark place. Transfer the ginger to a sterilized jar and pour the liquid completely over it. Refrigerate.

—Rachel Schneider

PICKLED DANDELION ROOTS

6–10 large late-fall or early
    spring dandelion roots,
    washed and chopped
3 garlic cloves, chopped

½ inch piece fresh ginger,
    minced
¼ cup tamari
Apple cider vinegar

Fill a quart jar with dandelion roots, garlic, ginger and tamari. Add enough apple cider vinegar to cover completely. Cover with a lid and let stand in the refrigerator 3–4 weeks. Put a piece of waxed paper between the lid and jar to keep the lid from rusting due to the acidic nature of the vinegar. Wonderful tasting alone, in salads, soups and stew. Best kept refrigerated.

—Suzanne Nagler

GREEN MANSION SALAD

1 head green cabbage	½ cup drained pineapple tidbits
½ cup green grapes, halved	½ cup shredded cucumber
1 Tbsp. lovage, cut fine	Lemon balm leaves

Remove center of cabbage, leaving outer leaves to form an edible bowl. Shred cabbage removed from the center and combine with rest of ingredients. Serve in the cabbage bowl. Chill. Garnish with lemon balm leaves. Serves 12.

—Judith Graves, Lambs & Thyme

The Cabbage Family

Cabbages (broccoli, Brussels sprouts, cabbage, cauliflower, collards, kale, kohlrabi, mustard greens and mustard seeds) have quite a reputation for healing a multitude of problems. Eating members of the cabbage or *brassica* family can lower "bad" cholesterol, improve colon function, fight yeast infections and heal gastrointestinal ulcers as well as provide protection from cancer and radiation. Drinking raw cabbage juice can heal ulcers and relieve acid indigestion. This is one food everyone should be eating more of.

MINT AND PEA SALAD

Thaw three 10-oz. packages of small peas (do not cook).
Mix together a dressing of:

2 Tbsp. fresh chives chopped small	3 Tbsp. minced fresh spearmint
1½ tsp. sugar	3 Tbsp. lemon juice
1½ cups chopped cucumber	¾ cup mayonnaise
	¾ cup sour cream

Fold into the peas and chill one hour to blend the flavors. Serves 12.

—Judith Graves, Lambs & Thyme

SPINACH AND FETA SALAD

Fresh spinach
Feta cheese
Black olives
Plum tomatoes, quartered
Apple slices

Mix ingredients and serve with Tarragon Mustard Salad Dressing (See page 67).

—Kiyra Page

CHICKEN SALAD WITH THYME AND RED ONION VINAIGRETTE

A zingy spring or summer salad, good warm or at room temperature. Pungent thyme is a natural accompaniment to sweet red onion in this salad. You can serve the salad warm or prepare it a few hours ahead of time and serve it at room temperature.

1 small red onion
½ head romaine lettuce
½ head red leaf lettuce
4 large skinless, boneless chicken breasts (about 1½ pounds) or 6 medium skinless, boneless chicken breasts

1 Tbsp. minced fresh thyme
Salt and fresh ground black pepper
⅓ cup olive oil
3 Tbsp. balsamic vinegar or red wine vinegar

Cut onion into paper-thin slices and separate into rings. Wash and spin-dry lettuces, tear leaves into pieces and chill. Cut chicken into 1-inch cubes and sprinkle with thyme, salt and pepper. Heat one half of the oil in a large frying pan over medium-high heat until hot, but not smoking. Add the chicken and sauté, stirring frequently, until just cooked through, about 5 minutes. Add the vinegar, stirring with a wooden spoon to deglaze the bottom of the pan. Remove pan from heat and stir in the onion and remaining oil. The recipe can be prepared to this point a few hours ahead. Set chicken and vinaigrette aside separately in covered containers. To serve, arrange chilled lettuce on salad plates and top with chicken and red-onion vinaigrette. Serves 4.

—PAULA WRIGHT, PONDLICK HERB FARM

Thyme

Any dish that can benefit from aromatic flavoring will be enhanced by the soothing, ripe fragrance of thyme. It can be used for flavoring cheeses, soups, stews, stuffings, meats, fishes, dressing, sauces and honey.

Thyme is a natural antibiotic capable of destroying infectious germs throughout the body. Thyme tea (steep 1 handful of fresh or 1 tablespoon dry thyme in 1 pint boiling water, covered, for ½ hour) can be used as a gargle for sore throats and coughs, a mouth wash for cold sores and tooth decay or a hot drink for fighting colds, influenza, fevers, allergies and asthma.

Thyme can be harvested all summer long, and either hung to dry or stripped from its stems and dried on trays. It can also be frozen.

CHICKEN SALAD

¼ cup mayonnaise	1 tsp. cumin
¼ cup plain yogurt	2 cups cooked chicken, cubed
½ Tbsp. lemon juice	½ cup slivered almonds
2 Tbsp. chopped fresh parsley	½ cup green grapes
2 tsp. coriander	Nasturtium blossoms

Combine mayonnaise, yogurt, lemon juice, parsley, coriander and cumin. Gently mix in chicken, and refrigerate at least 2 hours. Before serving, garnish with grapes, almonds and nasturtium blossoms. Serves 4.

—SUSAN WITTIG ALBERT, REPRINTED WITH PERMISSION
FROM *THYME AND SEASONS HERBAL TEAS.*

Edible Flowers

The saying "please don't eat the daisies" is not one to take seriously. Not only are daisies edible, but a whole lot of other flowers are as well. Nasturtiums and mustard flowers have hot spicy flavors; chives and onion blossoms lend their strong taste to salads, grains and other dishes; the gentle tastes of violets, pansies, borage and forget-me-nots taste and look great in salads, drinks, desserts and fruit dishes. Roses, pinks, bergamot, honeysuckle, jasmine and violets taste as good as they smell. Chrysanthemums and calendulas bring the sun into your food. Add just their petals to salads, soups and main dishes. Herb flowers, such as thyme, rosemary, dill, fennel, lavender and sage add more of the flavor and scent of the herb. Wildflowers are also edible: red clover, chicory, dandelion, elder flower, mallow, day lily, lilac and apple blossoms are just a few of the many that add delicious taste. Flowers can add beauty and flavor to food. *However, those who are susceptible to allergies should test a flower first by rubbing it on your wrist. If your skin reacts to it, do not eat it.*

SPRING GREENS WITH SHERRY VINAIGRETTE

Sherry vinaigrette:
1½ Tbsp. Sherry vinegar
1 tsp. Dijon mustard
½ tsp. salt
¼ tsp. ground black pepper

6 Tbsp. walnut oil
Salad:
2 quarts assorted salad greens: arugula, mache, oak leaf lettuce, baby mustard or frisée.

Mix vinegar, mustard, salt and pepper in a small bowl. Whisk in oil in a slow stream. Mix salad greens together in a serving bowl. Toss with vinaigrette. Serves 6.

—PAULA WRIGHT, PONDLICK HERB FARM

POTATO SALAD

5 cups potatoes
2 cups French sorrel
1 cup stinging nettles
¼ cup extra virgin olive oil

2–4 tsp. each fresh marjoram,
  basil and thyme
Salt and pepper to taste
Flowers for garnish

Cut the potatoes into cubes and cook with the jackets on. Cool. Steam the fresh nettles and sorrel until barely done, cool and cut into small pieces. Add the olive oil and stir in. Mince the fresh herbs (or use a mortar and pestle for dried herbs). Add salt and pepper. Garnish with flowers of calendula, pineapple sage, nasturtium, rosemary, borage or whatever is flowering. The sorrel gives the salad a bit of a sour taste, so it doesn't need vinegar, mustard or mayonnaise. Serves 8–10.

—CAROLE BROWN

MOCK POTATO SALAD

My recipes have been put together to help regain body chemistry balance according to the pH Balance Theory. I have used them all for many years. They are both unique and delicious, as well as very healthful.

1 head cauliflower
1 Tbsp. apple cider vinegar
4 boiled eggs, chopped
2 Tbsp. fresh parsley
½ medium onion, chopped

1 Tbsp. Lawry's seasoned salt
1 stalk celery, chopped
1 grated carrot
Paprika
Mayonnaise to moisten

Steam cauliflower until just tender; chop it up or mash it with a potato masher. Add remaining ingredients including mayonnaise according to preference. Blend together, sprinkle with paprika, and chill before serving. Serves 4.

—MICHAEL JONAS KAHN

GREEN RICE SALAD

6 oz. long grain brown rice
2 oz. wild rice
2 oz. fenugreek sprouts
1 bunch watercress
2 Tbsp. fresh parsley, chopped
2 Tbsp. fresh chives, chopped

4 Tbsp. olive oil
2 Tbsp. freshly squeezed lemon juice
Salt and pepper to taste
2 Tbsp. dry-roasted pine nuts or almonds

Cook the brown rice in boiling salted water for 40 minutes or until just tender. Rinse well with cold water. Drain and leave until it is cool. Cook the wild rice in boiling salted water for 30–40 minutes until fluffy and the grains pop open. Drain and set aside until it is cool. Put the brown rice into a serving bowl and stir in the wild rice and the fenugreek sprouts. Add the watercress leaves, parsley and chives. Mix the oil, lemon juice, salt and pepper; pour over the salad. Toss well. Sprinkle the roasted pine nuts or almonds on top. Serves 4.

Additional Suggestions: Use 8 oz. of long grain brown rice instead of the brown and wild rice. Substitute 2 Tbsp. of wine vinegar for the lemon juice. Sprinkle crumbled feta cheese on top.

—Sara Klein Ridgley

SNACKS

SWEET WILD PICKLES

Make a brine of

2 cups vinegar
1 cup sugar
1 cup water

Bring to a boil with 2 Tbsp. pickling spices. A nice wild blend might include spiceberries, sweetgale, mustard seed, sassafras root (Chinese ginger) and sweet cicely, all tied in a cloth bag. Simmer for 5 minutes. Add 3 cups wild vegetables (leeks, purslane stems, mallow seed wheels, cattail shoots, milkweed shoots, wild ginger root, sun tubers, ground cherries, ground nuts, solomon's seal roots, burdock root) and cook for 1 minute. The vegetables should remain crisp. Cool and refrigerate. It's best to make this several days ahead of time to allow the flavors to blend.

—Joyce Wardwell

To Help the Medicine Go Down

The Chi Ball recipe is one pleasant way to get your child to take his or her medicine. Simply knead each dose into a small ball. Other powdered herbs such as rosehips, catnip, fennel or anise can be added or substituted for the ginseng for a different flavor.

CHI BALLS

A simple but delicious energy snack that can be taken anywhere. Chi Balls, Zoom Balls, Crone Candy, Midnight at the Oasis Balls, Bee Pollen Energy Balls, Joy Balls. . . . It's amazing how many ball recipes there are—all with similar ingredients but different names—obviously a favorite snack among herbalists! With the common base a nut butter mixed with honey or molasses, the add-ins might include any one, two, three or four of the following: poppy seeds, carob powder, ginger, coconut, finely chopped dates or other dried fruits, ground nuts, cardamom powder, vanilla extract, essential oils or dried powdered herbs. Here is one delectable version.

2 cups tahini or almond butter
2 tsp. Siberian ginseng (powdered)
1 tsp. spirulina
2 tsp. bee pollen granules

1 tsp. flaxseed oil
1½ cups honey
½ cup raisins
½ cup crushed almonds

Mix first seven ingredients in a bowl. Roll into little balls or logs. Drop them in a bowl of crushed almonds and roll until completely covered. Place on wax paper and chill until ready to eat! These are so delicious! Kids love them as well. Makes about 20 balls.

—TERRA RENEAU

HERB ROASTED NUTS

These flavorful nuts are delicious on salads, casseroles, or as a snack. Experiment with different nut, herb and spice combinations. Try walnuts with Scarborough Fair Seasoning (page 90).

1 Tbsp. organic olive oil
1 Tbsp. melted organic butter or
  olive oil
2 cups nuts (fresh and organic
  are best)
1½–2 Tbsp. dried herbs or 4–6
  Tbsp fresh herbs

1 tsp. Hungarian paprika
1–1½ tsp. sea salt
2 tsp. vanilla-scented sugar (see
  recipe, page 189). Or use
  white, brown or natural cane
  sugar.

Preheat oven to 325° F. In a bowl, combine the melted butter or oil and nuts. Toss with a spoon to evenly coat. Blend herbs, paprika, salt and sugar. Sprinkle evenly over nuts and mix. Spread seasoned nuts in a single layer on a cookie sheet or glass casserole dish. Bake for 20–30 minutes, stirring every 8–10 minutes, making sure they do not burn. Serve warm or at room temperature. Store for up to two weeks in the refrigerator.

—SHARLEEN ANDREWS-MILLER

BEVERAGES

V-6 JUICE

3 cups tomato juice
2 Tbsp. each coarsely chopped fresh lamb's quarters, chickweed and
  sorrel
1 Tbsp. each coarsely chopped fresh dandelion, chive, and basil

Blend ingredients in an electric blender. Spike with a dash of tabasco, if
desired. Serves 2 or 3.

—JANICE SCHOFIELD

CAYENNE JUMP-START

Use this as a cold and flu remedy or an "eye-opener" in the morning.

1 cup chamomile tea
1 cup apple cider vinegar
2 tsp. cayenne powder
1 tsp. ginger powder
1 tsp. horseradish

Add vinegar, cayenne, ginger and horseradish to freshly brewed chamomile tea. Cover. Let steep for 10 minutes. Strain. Put 1 teaspoon to 1 tablespoon of the tea in tomato or vegetable juice. Take every 2–4 hours as needed for cold or flu. Take a smaller dose to get going in the morning instead of drinking coffee. This can be taken in grape juice also. This concoction can drive out a cold or flu bug within two days.

—KATHLEEN DUFFY

"COFFEE"

When I offer a cup of this brew to diehard coffee drinkers, they often prefer its flavor over real coffee. This brew has no caffeine and it is a lot less expensive as well.

Whole, organic soybeans
Dried dandelion root
Vanilla extract

In a 250° F oven roast 9 parts whole soybeans to 1 part dandelion root. Stir about every half hour to ensure an even roast. Roast until a rich dark brown but not black. This will take several hours. Cool and store in a glass jar. When ready to use grind in a coffee mill. For every Tbsp. of grounds, add ½ tsp. vanilla extract, blending thoroughly. Brew in the same proportions as regular coffee.

—JOYCE WARDWELL

CHOCOLATE COFFEE OR TEA

Before brewing coffee put six chocolate mint leaves (a type of mint) in the filter with the grounds. The coffee will smell and taste wonderful. Or, while brewing herbal tea, add three chocolate mint leaves to the cup.

—Jo-Ann Albano

CAFE DE OLLA

Other than tobacco, coffee may be one of our most used—and abused herbs. Used intelligently, however, coffee can serve as a remedy in certain situations. If your schedule is temporarily hectic, a cup of coffee can help you through the day. Most of us grew up smelling coffee brewing in the morning, and often we crave the familiar. Coffee shops are everywhere now and sometimes our health resolves are undermined by this temptation. There is a lot to be said about the healing effects of nurturing our need for comfort—even with an occasional cup of coffee. Cafe'de Olla is a recipe given to me by a friend who grew up in Guatemala. The name, literally translated, means coffee of the earthen pot. *Traditionally, it is served in earthen mugs. The spices aid in digestion, fight off a cold or flu and improve circulation.*

For 10 cups:
1 pod cardamom, split
½ tsp. cinnamon
¼ tsp. cloves
½ tsp. vanilla

Brew a full-flavored coffee of your choice with the first three spices. Add vanilla to the pot after brewing is completed and serve immediately. If desired, adjust recipe for fewer cups and use powdered cardamom instead. Serves 10.

—Tina Finneyfrock

HERBAL PUNCH

Blend equal amounts (about ½ oz. each) of dried lemon balm, chamomile, spearmint and red clover in a large glass jar. For each quart of punch, add 1 Tbsp. of herbal blend to 2 cups of boiling water. Steep for 5 to 7 minutes and strain. Mix with 2 cups of unsweetened apple, grape or berry juice.

This drink will keep your family healthy during cold season. It can be made into popsicles for children. Serves 6.

—Mary Bove

LEMON THYME ICE CUBES

Use these decorative and flavorful herbal ice cubes in iced teas, punch or sparkling drinks.

½ cup fresh lemon thyme flowers with 2–3 sets of leaves attached
1 handful fresh lemon thyme leaves

Brew 1–2 cups tea using the fresh thyme leaves (1 Tbsp. leaves to 8 oz. boiled water; cover, steep 10 minutes, strain and cool). Fill ice cube trays with cool lemon thyme tea. Arrange flowers in each cube, carefully. Freeze until needed.

—Kathleen Duffy

PINEAPPLE GARDEN PUNCH

Fill a pitcher with fresh bruised lemon balm and mint sprigs. Add a 46 oz. can of unsweetened pineapple juice, the juice of two lemons and 1 lemon, thinly sliced. Chill 8 hours, stirring occasionally and pressing herbs with a wooden spoon. At teatime, strain, pour into iced glasses and add a splash of sparkling water. Serves 6–8.

—SUSAN WITTIG ALBERT, REPRINTED WITH PERMISSION FROM
THYME AND SEASONS' HERBAL TEAS.

STRAWBERRY-APPLE-SPEARMINT JUICE

1 quart organic apple juice
1–2 drops spearmint essential oil or 1 cup fresh minced spearmint
2–3 cups fresh strawberries

If using fresh spearmint, soak it overnight in the apple juice and strain. Blend strawberries into the juice. Add essential oil. Garnish with fresh mint, a few whole berries and borage flowers. Serve iced. Serves 4.

—MAIA BALLIS, REPRINTED WITH PERMISSION FROM
SUN MOUNTAIN NATURAL FOODS COOKBOOK.

Have A Mint?

There are a great variety of mints, all of which make delicious additions to teas, drinks and desserts. Mint leaves can also be used in potpourri and as insect repellents. To varying degrees, mints are all digestive tonics, stimulating and easing digestion. They also are helpful in relieving headaches, colds and influenza.

PANSY PUNCH

½ cup water
1 cup sugar
1 cup strawberry syrup (see below)
2 cups orange juice

½ can crushed pineapple
½ cup maraschino cherries
½ quart charged water
Pansies for garnish

Boil water and sugar to a syrup, about 10 minutes. Add strawberry syrup,
orange juice and pineapple. Let stand ½ hour. Strain; add ice water to
make 1 gallon of liquid. Add cherries and charged water. Serve in a bowl
with a large piece of ice. Float pansies on top. Serves 25.

—JUDITH GRAVES, LAMBS AND THYME

STRAWBERRY SYRUP

6 lbs. fresh strawberries
2 oz. citric acid
1 quart water
3 lbs. sugar

Place strawberries in a deep glass or china bowl. Dissolve citric acid in water and pour over the fruit. Let stand for several hours. Strain, taking care
not to bruise the fruit, which would loosen the seeds. Now add sugar. Stir
the mixture well, using a silver spoon, until all the sugar is dissolved. Leave
uncovered for three days; then bottle and stopper. This syrup will not keep
long. Makes about 1 quart.

—JULIETTE DE BAIRACLI LEVY, REPRINTED WITH PERMISSION FROM
NATURE'S CHILDREN, ASH TREE PUBLISHING, 1997

WILD ROSE-ADE

1 cup wild rose petals, washed
2 cups water
½–1 cup raw sugar
Juice of 1 lemon, strained

Put washed rose petals in jar and pour water over them. Let stand overnight in the refrigerator. Shake every once in a while during the next day. Strain out the rose petals and put 1 cup of the rose water into a pan to heat (reserve the rest). Add sugar and warm until melted. Cool. Combine the strained lemon juice and the sugar mixture with the reserved rose water. Shake and enjoy! Serves 2.

—Feather Jones, Rocky Mountain Center for Botanical Studies

STRAWBERRY LEMON COLD ELIXIR

This mixture is incredibly delicious. It is not a good remedy for kids due to the alcohol content, but for adults it is relaxing and helps deal with the symptoms of coughs, flu and fever. It is best taken before bedtime or before a nap. Astragalus is a Chinese herb known for its immune-building properties.* The white cherry bark is antitussive (soothes a cough) and willow bark, an anti-inflammatory, helps ease headaches and bring down fevers.

If you decide to gather your own fresh barks, please do not strip them from the trunk of a living tree. Peel the barks from a twig or a branch so that the tree's life will not be in danger. Be sure to use only organic fruits. You do not want to make medicine with pesticide residues!

1 cup sliced organic lemons with peels left on	1 tsp. willow bark, cut and sifted
1 cup halved organic strawberries	1 tsp. wild cherry bark, cut and sifted
2 cups sugar	3 tsp. astragalus root
2 cups water	½ liter vodka
1 tsp. white oak bark, cut and sifted	2 Tbsp. vegetable glycerine

Combine the cut up lemons and strawberries with the sugar and water in a nonaluminum pot. Simmer until the sugar dissolves. Mix the barks and roots in a blender with the vodka. Combine the sugar and fruit with the vodka and barks in a large glass jar with a tight-fitting lid. Allow to sit for at least six weeks, strain and add the vegetable glycerine. Store in a dark glass bottle or in a dark cupboard. The dose is ¼ cup several times a day, as needed.

—ELLEN EVERT HOPMAN

---

*Instead of astragalus, echinacea angustifolia root or Siberian ginseng root can be used as an immune enhancer if desired, but they will have a stronger flavor.

FENNEL AND GINGER WINE

This sweet and spicy wine is also a digestive aid. It will help stimulate the appetite, promote digestion and alleviate gas.

1 lb. chopped ginger root	2 packages Red Star yeast
1 lb. fennel seeds	7 lb. raw honey
1 lb. wild carrot seeds	3 lb. dried apples
4 gallons water	

Add the roots and seeds to 2 gallons of boiling water. Reduce heat and simmer for 5 minutes. Let sit until room temperature. Strain and add enough water to make four gallons of liquid.

In a five-gallon bucket mix the water, yeast, honey and the fennel/ginger liquid. Stir to mix well. Cover with a cheesecloth, and let sit in a warm place for one week. Stir every day.

After one week, add the dried apples. Let sit until fermentation stops (No more bubbles will rise to the surface). This may take anywhere from 2–10 weeks, depending on the temperature. A warmer temperature speeds the process. Slowly pour or decant the wine, leaving the dregs behind. Bottle and store for 3–6 weeks before drinking.

—JOYCE WARDWELL

TEAS

Infusions. The general proportion of herb to water for tea-making purposes is 1 teaspoon dried herb (or 1 tablespoon fresh) to 1 cup water. A metal tea ball or strainer comes in handy for the one-cup-a-day crowd. If you will be drinking more than one cup a day, it makes sense to make a whole pot of tea. To do this, bring a quart of water to a boil, turn off the heat and place 4–6 tablespoons dried (or 4–6 handfuls of fresh) herb in the water. Stir and cover. Let steep at least 5–15 minutes before straining or leave it to steep all day if you wish. The longer it steeps, the stronger its medicinal value. (However, depending on the herbs used, it may also taste more like medicine!)

Decoctions. If your herbal tea blend contains roots, barks or other dense material (except for ginger, licorice or other highly aromatic roots), you will need to simmer the roots in water for 15–20 minutes before straining and drinking. You do not need to do this if you are using powdered roots.

Honey or sweetener can be added to taste while the tea is still hot. A thermos can keep your tea warm and available for sipping all day long, at work or play.

WARMING WINTER TEA

½ cup roasted dandelion root*
½ cup dried burdock root
1 quart water
Vanilla soy milk to taste
Maple syrup to taste

Simmer roots in water for 45–60 minutes. Stir in vanilla soy milk and maple syrup. Strain out roots and drink. This can be refrigerated and reheated. Serves 4.

—7SONG

*See next page for roasting instructions.

Dandelion Root

The scourge of the weekend gardener, dandelion has been cursed and sworn at for long enough. Don't weed your dandelions, eat them! With a handsome supply of vitamins and minerals, dandelion has provided food and medicine to people all over the world. One of the best herbal diuretics and bitters, dandelion has been used for kidney, liver and digestive disorders and is a good overall tonic for the digestive system. Be sure of identification, even with the dandelion. Harvest dandelions growing in unsprayed fields or yards only, not along roadsides. To use dandelion roots in winter teas, wash roots, dry with a towel, chop into small pieces and spread out on trays to dry in a warm place

Roasting Dandelion Roots

Dig dandelion roots (autumn is the best time), clean and chop into pieces, and dry roots until crisply dry—about two weeks. Spread on a cookie sheet and roast in a slow oven (250° F) for several hours, stirring occasionally, until they are dark brown. Check frequently. Grind the roots in a coffee grinder and store in a cool place.

LEMON-AID TEA

This pleasant tasting beverage tea is also a soothing digestive aid and well-supplied with vitamins A and C. Serve hot or iced with lemon thyme ice cubes. An excellent tea for herb tea novices or skeptical family members.

3 parts* lemon grass herb	2 parts orange peel
3 parts lemon verbena herb	1 part hibiscus flowers
3 parts lemon balm herb	1 part spearmint leaves
2 parts lemon peel	½ part licorice root

Mix well (all ingredients should be cut and dried). Store in glass jar away from heat, light and moisture. To make the tea, use 1–2 tsp. of the herb mixture per cup of boiling water. Steep, covered, for 5–15 minutes. Strain and sip slowly. No need to sweeten.

—KATHLEEN DUFFY

Tea Blends.

Mix these teas separately, place in glass jars and label. Thanks to JUDY DUNNING and BONNIE PASTOR, SOUTHWEST HERBS for the next five recipes.

SENSUAL-A-TEA

Some say that licorice and hibiscus are aphrodisiacs.

1 part licorice root, powdered
2 parts hibiscus
2 parts alfalfa (for energy)
1 part lemon verbena (for taste)
2 parts red clover (a stimulant)

*See page 37 for definition and instructions.

FEELGOOD TEA

4 parts chamomile (reduces headache pain, eases hangovers, improves digestion)

4 parts peppermint (same general effects as chamomile)

4 parts lemon verbena (for taste)

2 parts rosemary (to relax the body)

2 parts ginger root, powdered (eases headache pain, settles tummy)

2 parts rose hips, powdered (lots of vitamin C)

1 part fennel seed, powdered (settles tummy and soothes cramps)

STIMUAL-A-TEA

2 parts alfalfa (builds strength and energy)

2 parts red clover (for energy)

2 parts rose hips, powdered (more energy)

1 part ginger, powdered (even more energy and possible aphrodisiac)

2 parts lemon grass (for taste)

1 part rosemary (stimulates memory)

RELAX-A-TEA

2 parts chamomile (mild sedative, calmative)

1 part hibiscus (soothes the nerves)

2 parts red clover (relaxant)

1 part lemon grass (super lemon flavor)

CELEBRATION TEA

The herbs in this tea are for after a celebration. They bring you back down to earth, settle your tummy and ease your headache.

2 parts hibiscus
2 parts peppermint
1 part rose hips, powdered
1 part parsley
1 part alfalfa

What Is A Part?

How much a "part" is depends on how much of the tea you wish to have on hand. When first trying a blend, it is best to start with small amounts. If you want only one cup of tea to decide whether you like its taste, the *part* would be a *pinch*. If you would like to use the tea every day for a few days, use a *teaspoon*. Need a month's supply or more? Use with 1 *ounce* or ½ *cup*.

Those herbs that have stronger tastes are generally the ones with smaller parts. Their tastes should be considered when making larger amounts of a blend, and their parts adjusted to your own taste.

MIDNIGHT MADNESS

This blend is a serious herbal aphrodisiac and is best consumed less than two hours before retiring. The herbs also produce a great night's sleep. This blend tastes a little like beer.

2 parts damiana   ½ part hops
1 part oatstraw   ½ part cinnamon
1 part licorice root   1 part hibiscus

Brew tea for 10 minutes and enjoy.

—MICHELLE AND TOM LAWRENSON, THE HERBAL HARVEST

Buying Dried Herbs

Even if you are unfamiliar with the herb you are buying, it is a good idea to smell it, look at it closely and taste it before buying. Herbs have distinctive smells; they do not all have good smells, but they should smell strong when you buy them. Their colors should be bright and close to their original color. Their tastes should be strong and fresh. (Whether they taste good or bad to you is not an effective means of judgment as many herbs do not taste good.) If an herb does not meet these criteria then it is of poor quality and not worth using.

SAD TONIC

For those who live in the Northeast, or anywhere else that has precious few days of sunlight in the winter, Seasonal Affective Disorder (SAD) is a significant problem. The feelings of fatigue, depression and listlessness can last for months. Getting outside for half an hour per day, no matter what the weather, is a tremendous help, but often, not quite enough. I have found that the most reliable remedy for SAD is a tonic of nettles and lemon balm. Using ½ ounce of each, steep in 1 quart boiling water for 4 hours. Drink at room temperature throughout the day. Uplifted spirits return within a few days. This also makes a fine spring tonic.

—TINA FINNEYFROCK

CHANGE OF SEASONS BREW

This is a Native American brew that I use all year round. Try it and you'll never want coffee again.

   1 Tbsp. burdock root
   1 Tbsp. dandelion root
   1 Tbsp. chicory root
   1 Tbsp. yellow dock root

Add herbs to 5 cups of simmering water and continue to simmer for 20 minutes. Drink one cup in the morning. If you are pregnant, omit the yellow dock root. 4–5 servings.

—MARY PAT PALMER

Wildcrafted Herbal Teas

I have experimented heavily with a large variety of wildcrafted teas over the years, and tried them out on many acquaintances and students. Through this experience, I can confidently declare the following three teas as perennial favorites: leadplant, fireweed and mullein. These herbal brews seem to please just about any palate.

—Matthew Alfs

- **Leadplant,** a prairie-loving herb, yields a tea that was a favorite of the Fox Indians who used it medicinally to treat eczema and pinworms. It has a mild, soothing taste.

- **Fireweed,** an herb of burned-over ground, is an astringent and has been used to treat sore mucous membranes, diarrhea and inflammation in general, but it is perhaps most renowned as an overall tonic. It has a very refreshing taste.

- **Mullein,** a widespread weed of fields, roadsides and waste places, is another astringent herb and has been used by both herbalists and many American Indian tribes to heal asthma, other bronchial/pulmonary problems, adult diarrhea/colon problems and sinus blockage. It has a very soothing taste that is difficult to describe.

To make these teas, steep a tablespoon of fresh herb in a cup of boiling water, covered, for 10 minutes. Strain out the herb, if you wish to, and drink. Mullein should be strained through 1 or 2 coffee filters to remove the fine hairs of the plant.

ANTI-INFLAMMATORY TEA

Allopathic anti-inflammatories suppress rather than support the natural process of healing. Herbal anti-inflammatory teas gently encourage the body in its response to trauma or arthritis. This tea is especially soothing for arthritic pain. It is intended to assist the body during the transition to health.

1 cup meadowsweet herb
½ cup burdock root
½ cup black haw root
½ cup hawthorne leaves, berries
   and flowers

½ cup vitex berries
½ cup wild yam root
¼ cup sassafras root
⅛ cup licorice root

Mix together in a bowl and store in a glass jar in a cool dark place. To make a quart of the tea, put 1 tablespoon or more of the herb mixture into a quart mason jar (something that will take the heat), pour a quart of boiling water into the jar and cover. Let it steep for a minimum of 30 minutes or overnight. Strain and drink several cups a day.

—SAGE BLUE, WOLF HOWL HERBALS

Sometimes all there is left to do
Is to howl at the moon,
To add our voice to
The song of life,
To pour out our heart in
Mournful cry.

And our voice will be heard
And we will be filled.

—SAGE BLUE

"FOR THE BLUES" TEA

This is the very first tea blend I ever made. We still love it and use it regularly. It's great for stress, to gently relax you before bed, and is high in B-vitamins and trace minerals.

2 parts chamomile flowers
1 part borage
1 part stinging nettle
1 part skullcap

1 part peppermint
½ part rosehips
Stevia (a natural plant sweet-
    ener) to taste

I would suggest you experiment with stevia before committing it to a recipe. It is approximately 30 times sweeter than sugar, so a little goes a really long way. The first time I made this tea with stevia, it was absolutely undrinkable; a tiny pinch is all you need.

—Julie Manchester, Woodsong Herbals

Stevia

Also called sweet leaf and sweet herb, stevia has a sweetening power 30 times that of sugar and yet contains only one calorie for every 10 leaves. It is widely used as a sugar substitute throughout its native land, Central and South America. Japan has imported stevia since the 1970s and 11 Japanese companies are working on production and distribution of stevia-sweetened products. Japanese researchers claim stevia has no harmful effects, and 100 research papers back them up. Unfortunately, the FDA has not approved stevia for food use. While it is legal to sell stevia in the U.S., it is still considered an "unsafe food additive." Not many companies are likely to invest millions of dollars to win approval for a substance that, unlike artificial sweeteners such as NutraSweet, can't be patented.

Modern-day herbalists are using stevia as a sugar substitute for diabetics. It is sold in most health food stores and food cooperatives.

HAPPY HOUSE TEA

I originally blended this tea as a housewarming gift for friends. This is my favorite blend for a gentle, relaxing evening of peace, positive feelings and good cheer. For gift-giving, include a stainless steel mesh tea ball, tea-making directions and a unique tea mug. Use organic herbs whenever possible.

¼ cup of each of the following dried herbs (1 cup total):
Lemon balm
Spearmint
Oat straw
Chamomile

2 Tbsp. each of the following dried herbs (8 Tbsp. total):
rosehips
lavender
cinnamon chips
orange peel
1–2 tsp. of dried ginger for zing

Blend all ingredients thoroughly. Store in a clean, airtight glass jar away from heat, moisture and light for up to one year. Be sure to label. Use 1 heaping tablespoon of herb tea mix to 1 cup of boiling water. Allow the brew to steep (covered) for 5–10 minutes. Strain and sweeten with honey, if desired.

—SHARLEEN ANDREWS-MILLER

AFTER-BABY TEA

You could also call this tea Motherhood Tea or Vitali-Tea. The herbs in this tea blend are traditionally used to restore vitality, lift the spirits, tone and nourish the body, fill depleted reservoirs of strength (following birth) and gently calm and renew the system. Use organic herbs whenever possible. Fennel seeds (2 Tbsp., crushed) may be added if milk flow needs stimulating.

¼ cup each of the following dried herbs (1¼ cup total):
Red raspberry leaf
Lemon balm
Chamomile
Peppermint or spearmint
Oat straw

2 Tbsp. each of the following dried herbs (8 Tbsp. total):
Lavender flowers
Nettle leaves
Orange peel
Cinnamon chips

Blend all ingredients thoroughly. Store in a clean, airtight glass jar away from heat, moisture and light for up to one year. Be sure to label. Use 1 heaping Tbsp. of herb tea mix to 1 cup of boiling water. Allow the brew to steep (covered) for 5–10 minutes. Strain and sweeten with honey, if desired. Enjoy a relaxing cup of tea whenever you need a break.

—Sharleen Andrews-Miller

CALCIUM TEA

2 parts each:
    Chamomile
    Lavender
    Licorice
    Mullein
    Red raspberry
    Siberian ginseng
    Wood betony

1 part each:
    Alfalfa
    Catnip
    Comfrey leaf
    Lemon balm
    Skullcap
¼ part stevia, or to taste*

Combine dried herbs. Steep about 2 tsp. of the mixture in 1 cup of boiling water. Add more or less according to taste. This tea contains herbs that are high in calcium, magnesium and B and C vitamins. Some of the herbs are also used as nerve tonics, adaptogens, antispasmodics and to heal the liver.

—Carole Brown

*See page 42 for more about stevia.

DIPS, SANDWICHES & SPREADS

PESTO

2 cups fresh basil leaves
½ cup fresh parsley leaves
2–3 garlic cloves, peeled
½ cup olive oil

¼ cup roasted pine nuts or walnuts
¼ cup fresh Parmesan cheese

Purée the basil, parsley, oil and garlic in a blender or food processor. Add the nuts and the cheese and process until it is the desired consistency. This will keep in the refrigerator for one month if a thin film of oil is placed on top and tightly covered. It freezes well also. Use as a spread or dip for crackers or thin with more olive oil for use as a sauce or dressing. Yields approximately 1½ cups.

—Risa Mornis

WILD GREENS PESTO

The flavor of this pesto varies depending upon the proportion of basil leaves to wild greens, the time of the year that the greens are harvested e.g., dandelion greens are more bitter after flowering, and the types of greens that you use e.g., sheep sorrel imparts a tart, lemony flavor while lamb's quarters taste more like spinach. Experiment and find the flavor you like best.

3 cups lightly packed leaves (a combination of basil and wild greens such as lamb's quarters, plantain, dandelion, sheep sorrel, amaranth.) You may want to start with 1½–2 cups of basil leaves with the balance a combination of wild greens.

3 cloves garlic
½ cup cold-pressed, extra virgin olive oil
½ cup pine nuts, walnuts or almonds
1 Tbsp. dulse flakes
¼ tsp. each salt and freshly ground black pepper

Put all ingredients into a food processor or blender. Process until smooth. Adjust salt and pepper amounts for your own taste. This is delicious on bread, crackers or steamed vegetables such as summer squash or pasta.

Wild greens pesto freezes well so that you can enjoy a wonderful remembrance of your summer foraging in the middle of winter. If you do not freeze it but do not use it up the day that it is prepared, store it in a covered glass bowl in the refrigerator. Pour a little extra olive oil over the top of the pesto first. This keeps it from discoloring. Makes 1–2 cups.

—BARBARA NARDOZZI

Freezing Pesto

This is the best way to have fresh-tasing pesto long after the garden is covered in snow. Pour pesto into ice cube trays and freeze. When cubes are solid, remove and put in an airtight freezer bag. Each pesto cube is just the right size for one serving.

JO-ANN ALBANO, LADYBUG KNOLL

NESTO (NETTLE PESTO)

1 cup extra virgin olive oil
½ cup pine nuts
6–8 cloves garlic
½ cup Parmesan cheese
4 cups lightly steamed nettles, drained (*Urtica* species)

Blend oil, pine nuts and garlic in blender until creamy. Add cheese and nettles and continue blending to make a green paste. Extra olive oil may be added to make this thinner for use as a salad dressing or pasta sauce. Thick nesto can be used as a paté for crackers. Adjust ingredients according to your taste buds with more or less garlic, cheese and nuts. Makes 2–3 cups.

—JANICE SCHOFIELD

SPINACH OR STINGING NETTLE DIP

1 bunch spinach or stinging nettles or a mixture of both. (Other
    fresh tender greens such as chickweed, lamb's quarters or culti-
    vated greens can be used as well.)
8 oz. cream cheese, neufchatel or cottage cheese
1 large clove garlic
1 tsp. lemon juice
2–4 oz. feta cheese

Wash the spinach/nettles well and steam until well-wilted. Remove
steamer from above boiling water and let the greens cool. Meanwhile, put
the cream cheese and the garlic in a bowl or a food processor and blend
well. Squeeze out extra water from the greens (drink or save for soup) and
add a few greens at a time to the cream cheese while the blades are running. Add the lemon juice towards the end. Crumble the feta and gently
mix it in by turning the motor off and on a few times. I like to leave some
small chunks of feta in the mixture. Serve with good chewy bread, crunchy
crackers or vegetable crudités. Or serve with steamed artichokes for a real
digestive boost.

—CASCADE ANDERSON GELLER

SPRING HERB DIP

3 cloves garlic, pressed
¼ cup fresh chives
¼ cup fresh lovage
2 Tbsp. fresh tarragon
10.5 oz. package soft tofu

2 Tbsp. olive oil
3 Tbsp. white wine vinegar
Salt and freshly ground pepper
    to taste
Lovage leaves for garnish

Process all in a food processor until smooth. Serve as dip with raw vegetables or with crackers. Garnish with lovage leaves. Yields 1½ cups.

—JILL YECK, PECONIC RIVER HERB FARM

Nettle

A large number of the recipes in this book contain nettle. It is undoubtedly a favorite among herbalists. Its high vitamin and mineral content and its tonic and medicinal properties, as well as its mild and delicious flavor, make it popular as both medicine and food. It is particularly high in calcium and iron.

The sting of fresh nettle feels similar to a jellyfish sting—a burning, tingling, itching sensation. The stinging hairs on the leaves contain formic acid, which does not survive heat; thus cooked nettles are stingless and deliciously edible. Nettle is a spring pot herb. Do not eat it once it is over six inches tall. Some nettle enthusiasts may eat nettles throughout the summer by harvesting only the tips of pre-flowering plants. To avoid the sting while harvesting, use rubber gloves. Nettles will absorb almost all the minerals—good or bad—present in the soil, so harvest only in clean areas.

Medicinally, nettle is used in the treatment of skin diseases, allergies, arthritis, infertility, as a tonic during pregnancy and as a diuretic. The best time to harvest it for medicinal purposes is when its tiny green flowers are in bloom.

DANDELION DIP

¼ cup yogurt
½ cup cottage cheese
1 cup dandelion greens
Garlic powder
Salt to taste

Mix cottage cheese and yogurt (or combine in blender). Mince greens well and add to yogurt/cheese mixture. Season with garlic powder and salt. Serve with oat cakes or crackers. Makes 1 cup.

—Feather Jones, Rocky Mountain Center for Botanical Studies

HILBA

This fenugreek dip or condiment is bitter in taste, and best eaten with soup or as a condiment to vegetables. It is a staple food in Yemen and for all Yemenite Jews in Israel.

¼ cup fenugreek seeds (see next page)
2 cups water
Juice of ½ large lemon or one whole small lemon
¼ tsp. salt (or to taste)

Grind the fenugreek seeds in a coffee mill (or a seed grinder) until powdered. Put in a large bowl and add 2 cups of water (more if needed), lemon juice and salt. Stir vigorously with a fork, beating lightly. Let stand for about ½ an hour at room temperature. Using the fork, beat again, more vigorously this time. The fenugreek will have formed into a mousse-like consistency, which, while beating, will froth up like beaten egg white. Adjust flavor with more salt/lemon juice and store in refrigerator. Makes about 2 cups.
Additional suggestions: Chopped coriander leaves (cilantro) as well as a hot salsa are delicious mixed with this condiment.

—Sara Klein Ridgley

Fenugreek

Fenugreek is a highly valued herb in India and in the Middle East. It is considered of prime importance to balance blood sugar levels and provide a bitter taste to enhance digestion, supporting the metabolism of carbohydrates into energy. Soaking 1 tsp. of the seeds overnight in water and drinking the water in the morning has been used by herbalists and Ayurvedic physicians for generations to detoxify the liver.

In the 1950s, the entire Jewish population of Yemen was transported almost overnight to Israel due to persecution. This ethnic group, now totally assimilated into the rest of the Israeli population, brought with them some very interesting eating habits. Fenugreek and garlic as well as leafy greens are extensively used in their diet. Not surprisingly, the entire group had no signs or history of either diabetes or heart disease. However, since that time, most of them have totally adapted to the common Israeli diet, and now, alas, they have both these diseases just like the native-born Israeli population.

—SARA KLEIN RIDGLEY

ZA'ARTA

This is a special traditional condiment of the Bedouin Arabs.

To every handful of dried thyme add ½ cup of roasted sesame seeds (whole or ground), 2 tsp. of powdered coriander seed and a little salt. Mix well.
    Za'arta is eaten on bread spread with olive oil to hold the condiment.

—JULIETTE DE BAIRACLI LEVY, REPRINTED WITH PERMISSION FROM *NATURE'S CHILDREN*, ASH TREE PUBLISHING

SPICED TOFU (MOCK EGG SALAD)

¼ cup dried parsley (or ½ cup fresh)
2 Tbsp. sesame salt (gomashio)
2 Tbsp. nutritional yeast
2 tsp. garlic powder

1 tsp. each dillweed, paprika and black pepper
½ tsp. each turmeric, celery seed, caraway seed and stevia powder

Grind the herbs together in an herb mill or dry blender and add to the ingredients below in a food processor with chopper blade:

1 pound tofu (approximately)
1 green pepper seeded and chopped or ½ cup nopales
¼ cup eggless mayonnaise
2 Tbsp. prepared mustard

2 minced scallions
1 celery stalk chopped
1 Tbsp. tamari or miso paste (or sea salt to taste)
½ dill pickle (optional)

Use as a squash blossom filling and serve remainder mounded in the center of a platter with stuffed blossoms on top. This is also a great sandwich spread. Makes about 2 cups.

—MAIA BALLIS, REPRINTED WITH PERMISSION FROM
SUN MOUNTAIN NATURAL FOODS COOKBOOK

TOFU CURRY

In a cast iron skillet simmer 2 to 3 minutes:

1 Tbsp. olive oil
1½ tsp. onion powder
1 tsp. curry powder
½ tsp. garlic powder

Add 1 cup of water to dissolve spices. Pour into a blender and add:

¼ cup light cream cheese or feta cheese
2 tsp. miso paste (or soy sauce)
16 oz. tofu

Use as a dip for veggies or as a sauce for pocket bread filled with cactus pads, black or green olives, sprouts and feta cheese. Makes 2–3 cups.

—Maia Ballis, reprinted with permission from *Sun Mountain Natural Foods Cookbook*

Gomashio

This Oriental combination of sesame seeds and salt is used like salt at the table and provides delicious flavor with much less sodium and much more calcium.

4 Tbsp. sesame seeds
1 tsp. salt

Toast seeds in a dry skillet until just brown. Use low heat and stir constantly to prevent burning. Grind in a blender or mortar until fine. Add the salt and grind a few seconds longer to mix. Makes ¼ cup. See page 142 for another version of gomashio.

Making Your Own Mustards

Mustard flavors will mellow and taste very different after several days. To grind seeds, use a spice grinder, coffee grinder or mortar and pestle. If mustard is too soupy, cook over low heat until it thickens. Add vinegar or very small amounts of any other liquid if mustard is too stiff. Following are four of my favorite mustard recipes.

—Christine McKenna, Herbal Earth

Lemon Thyme Mustard

Mild and lemony.

¼ cup mustard seed
¼ tsp. mustard powder
2 Tbsp. lemon juice
1 Tbsp. sugar
¼ tsp. salt

¾ cup water
1 tsp. dried lemon thyme (or regular thyme)
2 Tbsp. white vinegar

Grind the mustard seeds until they look like coarse cornmeal. In a small saucepan, mix them with the mustard powder, lemon juice, sugar and salt. Stir in the water and then place over medium heat. Bring to the simmering point. Cook 5 minutes while stirring. Take off heat, add thyme and let cool. Add vinegar or a small amount of another liquid if the mustard is too stiff. Pour into a jar and keep refrigerated. This is good with chicken, fish and steak. When freshly made this mustard is rather strong and pungent. After a day or so it blends and tastes very lemony. Makes about 1 cup.

TARRAGON MUSTARD

Pungent, strongly flavored.

¼ cup mustard seed   1 Tbsp. brown sugar
½ tsp. powdered mustard   ½ tsp. salt
½ cup dry wine   2 tsp. dried tarragon
¼ cup red wine vinegar

Grind mustard seeds until they look like coarse cornmeal. Mix with mustard powder, wine and vinegar in a small saucepan. Stir over low heat until smooth. Add sugar and salt. Simmer for 20 minutes or until mixture thickens well. Stir in tarragon. Use right away as a warm sauce or cool and refrigerate. It thickens as it cools. You can substitute oregano or basil for tarragon. Makes about ¾ cup.

HOT HONEY MUSTARD

Very hot!

4 Tbsp. mustard powder
2 Tbsp. water
1 tsp. vinegar
1 Tbsp. olive oil
2 Tbsp. honey

Mix the mustard to a stiff paste with the water and vinegar. Stir in the oil until the mixture is smooth; stir in the honey. Pour into a jar. Makes ⅓ cup.

MAPLE MUSTARD

Sweet with a good texture.

¼ cup mustard seed
3 Tbsp. mustard powder
2 Tbsp. white vinegar
½ cup pure maple syrup
Pinch of salt

Grind mustard seed until of a medium coarse texture. In a small saucepan mix all ingredients. Cook over low heat until it thickens, approximately 15 minutes, stirring continuously. Put in a jar and refrigerate. Great with ham, sausage and pork. Makes about ⅔ cup.

EASY HOMEMADE MUSTARD

A sharp, all-purpose mustard to spice up a sandwich.

3 Tbsp. dry mustard powder   1½ tsp. white wine
1 tsp. water   2 tsp. honey
1 tsp. olive oil   ¼ tsp. turmeric

Thin the dry mustard with the water and let set for 10–15 minutes. Then add oil and mix. Stir in the remaining ingredients. Makes ⅓ cup.

—SUSAN WITTIG ALBERT, REPRINTED WITH PERMISSION FROM *MARVELOUS MUSTARDS AND CURIOUS CURRIES*

SANDWICHES

There are a large number of healthy whole grain breads on the market to choose from. Avoid white bread, which has almost no nutritional value. Select breads made with sprouted grains of rye, oats and millet as well as whole wheat. Eating wheat products only sometime leads to wheat allergy.

Tasty Sandwich Combinations

1. Dilled cream cheese, cucumbers and chickweed on rye bread.

2. Baked tofu, mustard spread and purslane or chickweed on whole wheat bread.

3. Hummus (chickpeas, sesame butter, lemon juice, garlic and spices processed into a paste), olives and lamb's quarters in a pita.

4. Tofu "egg" salad, (tofu mixed with mayonnaise, mustard, dill and/or other herbs and spices), cucumbers and watercress or parsley on any bread.

—Risa Mornis

SPRING DELIGHT SANDWICH

Place ripe avocado slices on whole wheat cinnamon-raisin bread. Add raw goat cheddar cheese. Toast until cheese is melted, then add fresh wild greens such as dandelions, chickweed, violet leaves or garlic mustard. Top with burdock vinegar. Toast for one more minute.

—Robin Rose Bennett

Burdock Vinegar

Fill a clean jar to the top with freshly harvested, cleaned and chopped burdock root. (See page 143 for when to harvest burdock.) Cover to the top with apple cider vinegar or wine vinegar. Let steep for 3 to 6 weeks or more. Strain and use on salads or steamed vegetables.

WILDFLOWER PITAS

1 Tbsp. lemon juice
1 Tbsp. maple syrup
1–2 cups assorted flowers (violets, field pansies, wood sorrel, wild mustard, redbud)

2 pita breads
Mixed salad greens (corn salad, cress, chickweed, lamb's quarters, violet leaves, sheep sorrel)

Mix lemon juice and maple syrup and pour over flowers. Cut pitas in half. Stuff a layer of greens on inside of pita. Top with flowers and serve.

—Vickie Shufer

Gathering Wildflowers

Select the cleanest, freshest, most bug-free flowers for eating, and cut them carefully to encourage the new buds still on the plant to bloom. Gather them just before eating, if possible, and spray them lightly with water. If they are to be stored, put them in a plastic, wax or woven bag and keep them moist.

Violet

All varieties of the violet—wild or cultivated—are edible.
The leaves and flowers can both be eaten, although the
leaves are used more for medicine. The flowers are
sweet, often used in desserts, drinks and salads. The
leaves are used as a tea for relief of respiratory conges-
tion and externally as a poultice for breast cysts. The leaves
and flowers together make a cooling, soothing tea for calm-
ing, easing stress, as well as aches and pains at the end of a long
day. *Caution:* Externally, the leaves can cause a rash on the skin
of allergy-prone individuals.

JAM AND JELLY

ROSEHIP AND APPLE JAM

2 lb. ripe rosehips
2 lb. sour apples
3 pints water
1¾ lb. sugar

Wash the rosehips and place in a pan with the water. Bring to a boil and
simmer until soft and pulpy. Break the fruit down with a spoon, then
strain the pulp through a jelly bag overnight. Discard pulp and save the
juice. Peel the apples and cut up roughly. Place in a pan with just enough
water to prevent burning and cook until soft. Add the rosehip juice and
the sugar, dissolve carefully, then allow to come to the boil. Boil briskly
until setting point is reached. Pour into hot sterilized jars. Cool for a few
minutes before covering with melted paraffin wax and sealing. Makes
about 3 pints.

—CAROLINE HOLMES

QUEEN ANNE'S LACE JELLY

7 cups water
30 large Queen Anne's lace flower heads
2 packages Sure-Jell (or pectin made from apples)
7½ cups sugar (or substitute honey for syrup)

Boil water. Steep flowers in water for 10 minutes. Strain and measure 6 cups. Add Sure-Jell. Bring to a boil and add sugar while stirring. Stir at a boil for one minute. Skim and pour into jars. Place one small Queen Anne's lace flower head in the top of each jar at this point (it will set in top and look great when opened). Seal in canner. Makes 3 pints.

—Pat Chichon

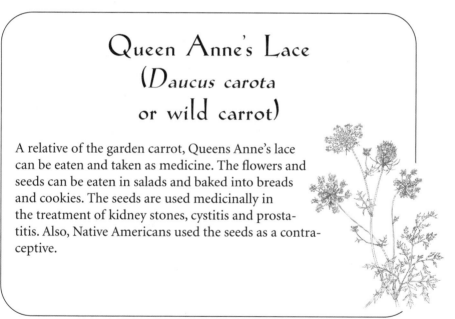

Queen Anne's Lace (Daucus carota or wild carrot)

A relative of the garden carrot, Queens Anne's lace can be eaten and taken as medicine. The flowers and seeds can be eaten in salads and baked into breads and cookies. The seeds are used medicinally in the treatment of kidney stones, cystitis and prosta-titis. Also, Native Americans used the seeds as a contra-ceptive.

VINEGARS & DRESSINGS

VINEGARS

There seems to be as many ways to make vinegar as there are herbalists. I have found only one fast rule: cover the herbs completely with vinegar, so that they do not mold. When first experimenting with vinegars and their tastes, it is best to follow a recipe. From there, decisions can be made according to your own taste buds and convenience. Basic guidelines for making those decisions are offered here.

- Herbs that contain volatile oils, such as basil, oregano, rosemary and other strong-smelling and sharp-tasting herbs, should be used in small amounts when first experimenting with flavors (start with no more than 1 cup fresh or ½ cup dried herb per quart of vinegar). Wild greens, such as dandelion, nettle, chickweed and lamb's quarters, can be added for extra nutrition. If the vinegar tastes too strong, you can dilute it by adding more vinegar.

- Cover the herbs with vinegar. You can use any kind of vinegar, but herbalists tend to prefer the ones with extra health value: apple cider vinegar, red wine vinegar or rice vinegar. White wine vinegar may be preferred for its ability to bring out the bright colors of herbs such as violet or chive blossoms. Do not boil your vinegar. This will ruin it. You may heat it, if you wish, to enhance the flavor of the herbs. However, just setting your vinegar in a sunny spot will do the job.

- Cap with a cork, plastic lid or glass lid. Do not use metal as the vinegar will corrode the lid. Plastic wrap under a metal lid can be used if nothing else is available.

- Let sit in a warm spot for anywhere from 2 to 6 weeks. The flavor of the vinegar will strengthen the longer the herbs steep. Check after a few days to be sure no herbs are sticking up above the vinegar. Add more vinegar if necessary. Strain out the herbs by pouring the vinegar through cheesecloth or fine sieve or leave the herbs in and use them as you use the vinegar, adding them into your salads and cooking. The vinegar will keep up to a year or more if stored in a cool place.

- Favorite wild herbs for making into vinegars are violet, chives, nettles, mugwort, dandelion roots and leaves.

DANDELION BALSAMIC VINEGAR

This is especially good on steamed greens with toasted sesame seeds. Dandelion is very high in vitamins and minerals. A half-cup of steamed greens can contain more than 12,000 units of vitamin A. The vinegar also makes minerals such as calcium and iron more available in the foods we put it on. Be sure to harvest dandelion away from roads or sprayed areas.

Whole cleaned dandelion roots and leaves
Balsamic vinegar

Coarsely chop dandelion and loosely pack it into a jar so that it almost reaches the top. Fill the jar with vinegar. Place a piece of plastic wrap over the top of the jar and put a lid on over the plastic. You don't need the plastic if your jar lid is sealed with one of the food grade sealants so that it resists the rusting action of the vinegar. Let it sit in a dark place at room temperature for two weeks. Shake daily. Strain through cheesecloth and store in refrigerator.

—COLETTE GARDINER

"COLD KICKER" CRYSTAL-INFUSED MEDICINAL HERBAL VINEGAR

Take one tablespoon of this delicious herbal vinegar when you start to feel the first signs of a cold or flu. It is even better when taken daily as a preventative.

1 Tbsp. whole black peppercorns
5 fresh tarragon sprigs
8 cloves peeled garlic
4 cups cider vinegar
1 amethyst crystal

Fill a glass jar or bottle with the peppercorns and tarragon. Nick the garlic and add. Next, drop an amethyst crystal into the jar and cover entire contents with the vinegar. Be sure that everything is completely submerged in the vinegar so that no bacteria can form. Let sit in a cool, dark place for 6 weeks. Then it is ready to use to fight infections and colds. The amethyst crystal protects the throat, lungs and respiratory system. Makes 4 cups.

—RACHEL SCHNEIDER, FLOWER POWER HERBALS

HOT CHILE VINEGAR

This makes a colorful gift and adds zest to your cooking. Into a pretty, narrow-necked bottle (8- to 10-oz. size) place 3 to 4 small, cayenne peppers (fresh or dried), 1 or 2 small cloves of garlic, 2 sprigs of purple basil, 1 whole clove and a few peppercorns. Fill to cover all herbs with red wine vinegar, cork and place in a sunny window for one week. Never boil vinegar before adding it to your herbs. This will send the oils of the herbs up in the steam leaving you with no herbal essence left for flavor. We often dip the top of the bottle into melted paraffin to seal the cork, tie on a raffia bow, make a tag and give as a hostess or holiday gift. Makes 1 cup.

—JUDY DUNNING AND BONNIE PASTOR, SOUTHWEST HERBS

HOT AND SPICY VINEGAR

Make this spicy vinegar after the summer's harvest to have for the long winter months ahead. Packed full of cayenne peppers and garlic, this vinegar will keep your heart strong and your circulatory system moving all winter.

What you will need:
   Glass jar with tight-fitting lid
   Cayenne peppers (fresh and in different colors if possible; I like
      green, orange and red).
   Fresh-peeled cloves of garlic
   Pure apple cider vinegar

Clean glass jar with hot soapy water and rinse. Fill with peppers and garlic, arranging them in an artistic way. Warm apple cider vinegar to room temperature and pour gently over peppers and garlic until they are covered. Cap and label. Let sit in a warm place out of direct sunlight for 3 to 4 weeks. Use on salads, stir fries or on anything needing a little extra spice.

—SONIA POITRAS, EARTH SPIRIT HERBALS

GARLIC AND HERB VINEGAR

   3 pressed garlic cloves
   1 Tbsp. oregano
   1 Tbsp. chopped chives
   2 cups white wine vinegar

Put garlic and herbs in a glass or cork-stoppered bottle or a recycled salad dressing jar. Add white wine vinegar, and let sit at least one week or up to 6–8 weeks. Strain and rebottle. Makes 2 cups.

—HARVEST MCCAMPBELL

Dressings

Roasted Sesame Milk Thistle Salad Dressing Mix

1 cup sesame seeds
1 cup milk thistle seeds
⅛ cup sea salt

Roast all ingredients in an iron skillet on medium heat until sesame seeds are brown. For a salad dressing, add 2–4 tablespoons to ½ cup unpasturized apple cider vinegar and ½ cup olive oil. Or simply sprinkle the mix on soup or bread.

—Bryan Ray Keith

Milk Thistle

Milk thistle is a highly regarded liver herb, one so powerful it can help the body rebuild a damaged liver. Renowned for its success against amanita mushroom poisoning, drug addictions, hepatitis and other liver disorders, milk thistle seeds can also be used preventively to protect the liver from toxins. Milk thistle seeds can be eaten or taken as tinctures or pills and must be taken daily for a month or more to show positive results.

Milk thistle has a rich tasty flavor and is very nutritious. It contains starch, protein and linoleic acid, an essential fatty acid. The seeds can be ground in a coffee grinder and eaten by the teaspoonful; the young tender leaves and stalks, stripped of their prickers, can be eaten raw or cooked; and the heads can be cooked like their relative, the artichoke. See page 142 for another milk thistle recipe.

LOW-FAT GARLIC
AND HERB SALAD DRESSING

6 cloves garlic
½ cup water
1 Tbsp. olive oil
8 sprigs fresh cilantro
2 sprigs fresh tarragon

2 tsp. herb vinegar
1 tsp. honey
⅛ tsp. liquid lecithin
¾ tsp. arrowroot
1 pinch herb salt*

Press garlic into food processor. Add remaining ingredients and process until herbs are finely chopped. Pour into small skillet, turn heat on low and stir until thickened. Makes about ¾ cup.

—HARVEST MCCAMPBELL

TARRAGON MUSTARD SALAD DRESSING

1 tsp. olive oil
2 Tbsp. tarragon or balsamic vinegar
2 tsp. Dijon or stone ground mustard

Mix into salad, tossing lightly. Serves 1.

—KIYRA PAGE

*See recipe on next page

Herb and Garlic Salt

½ cup sea salt
3 pressed garlic cloves
¼ cup fresh herbs, woody parts discarded. Basil, chives, marjoram,
oregano, savory, tarragon and thyme are a few choices.

Place ingredients in a food processor and process until smooth or
crush together with a mortar and pestle. Dry in an oven on low heat
with the oven door slightly ajar, stirring frequently, until herbs are
crisp. Put in a shaker bottle. Use in place of salt in recipes.

—HARVEST McCAMPBELL

THREE SEAWEED DRESSING

2 sheets toasted nori seaweed   ¼ cup olive oil
2 heaping Tbsp. kelp powder   ⅛ cup tamari
2 Tbsp. dulse granules   2 Tbsp. toasted sesame oil
1 cup unpasturized cider vinegar   ⅛ cup water

Mix all ingredients together in a blender. This dressing is high in vitamins
and iodine. Makes 1½ cups.

—BRYAN RAY KEITH

RED CHILE DRESSING

3 large dried chiles (Anaheim,
    Ancho, Chipotle, New Mex or
    Pasilla)
⅔ cup water
6 Tbsp. apple cider or red wine
    vinegar

2 Tbsp. sugar
1 Tbsp. chopped fresh ginger
2 Tbsp. extra virgin olive oil

Rinse the chiles and remove all seeds and stems. Set water to boil and chop chiles into medium-sized pieces. Drop chile pieces into boiling water, remove from heat and let set 5 minutes. Combine all ingredients in a blender or food processor, and process until puréed. Refrigerate and use within a week. Makes 1 cup.

—BONNIE PASTOR & JUDY DUNNING, SOUTHWEST HERBS

SUN-DRIED TOMATO VINAIGRETTE

¼ cup balsamic vinegar
1 medium shallot, minced
8 sun-dried tomatoes packed in
    oil, drained
6 large leaves of fresh basil

1 medium clove garlic
2 Tbsp. red wine vinegar
¼ cup water
½ cup olive oil

Bring balsamic vinegar and minced shallot to boil in a nonreactive saucepan. Simmer until reduced to 2 tablespoons, about 2 minutes. Transfer to a food processor. Add next five ingredients; process until solids are minced. Add the oil in a slow, steady stream. Makes ¾ cup.

—PAULA WRIGHT, PONDLICK HERB FARM

ECHINACEA/SHEEP SORREL DRESSING

3 Tbsp. each powdered echinacea root and sheep sorrel
1 cup unpasturized cider vinegar
½ cup olive oil
3 Tbsp. lemon or lime juice

1 Tbsp. garlic granules
1 Tbsp. onion granules
4 big pinches parsley flakes
Salt and pepper to taste

Blend mixture and set out overnight in sealed jar. This is a tangy immune stimulant. Makes about 1½ cups.

—BRYAN RAY KEITH

SHAR'S RASPBERRY POPPY SEED VINAIGRETTE

Feel free to adjust proportions to satisfy your taste buds. This dressing is wonderful on a wild weed salad (dandelion, chickweed, sorrel, watercress, miner's lettuce, etc.) topped with crumbled feta cheese, sprinkled with fresh dill and herb-roasted walnuts and garnished with fresh violets. This recipe uses flaxseed oil (high in beneficial essential fatty acids) along with immuneenhancing, antioxidant ingredients such as garlic and vitamin C-rich fresh lemon juice and raspberries.

⅓ cup white wine raspberry vinegar*

⅓ cup balsamic and/or red wine vinegar

¼ to ⅓ cup organic extra virgin olive oil

¼ cup flaxseed oil (or substitute an olive or nut oil)

¼ to ⅓ cup honey

¼ cup fresh chopped chives

1–3 Tbsp. fresh minced garlic

2 Tbsp. fresh organic lemon juice

1 Tbsp. poppy seeds

1 tsp. dried mustard

¼–½ tsp. mace (add spicy flavor)

¼ tsp. Hungarian paprika

Freshly ground black pepper to taste

Mix all ingredients and keep refrigerated. Best if allowed to mellow a few hours before using. Olive oil will solidify slightly in the refrigerator, so allow vinaigrette time to come to room temperature before serving. Makes about 1½ cups.

—SHARLEEN ANDREWS-MILLER

*See recipe on next page

Raspberry Vinegar

In June I harvest my raspberries to make vinegar that lasts all year. After cleaning, I smash the raspberries and add them to white wine vinegar. (You can also use red wine, apple cider or balsamic vinegar, but white shows the vivid raspberry color best.) Proportions vary, but approximately 1 part berries to 4 to 6 parts vinegar. Keep at room temperature, shaking daily for 7 to 10 days; strain, then refrigerate. I sometimes leave the berry pulp in and have had no problems; just be sure to refrigerate. Try experimenting with wild blackberries, Salal berries or Oregon grape berries for wild berry-flavored vinegars.

—SHARLEEN ANDREWS-MILLER

NON-VINEGAR HERBAL SALAD DRESSING

1 tsp. dried marjoram
1 tsp. dried chervil
1 tsp. dried thyme
½ tsp. dried field mint
¼ tsp. dried tarragon

10 Tbsp. virgin olive oil
4 tsp. fresh lemon juice
3 cloves raw garlic, minced finely
1 tsp. sea salt (or to taste)
Freshly ground black pepper

Combine dried herbs by grinding with a mortar and pestle. Add olive oil, lemon juice and minced garlic, plus salt and pepper to taste. Refrigerate overnight to allow the herb flavors to meld. This can be used as a dressing for wild greens, or as a marinade for chicken or fish

—MARY AND GREGORY WULFF-TILFORD, ANIMAL'S APAWTHECARY

GREEN HERB DRESSING

¾ cup mayonnaise
1½ tsp. basil
1 tsp. dillweed
2 Tbsp. chopped chives
2 tsp. crushed tarragon

¼ tsp. paprika
2 Tbsp. chopped parsley
½ tsp. seasoned salt
1 tsp. thyme
⅔ cup plain yogurt

Combine all ingredients in a small bowl and mix well. Cover and refrigerate overnight. Makes 1½ cups.

—MICHAEL JONAS KAHN

BASIL WALNUT DRESSING

⅓ cup lemon juice
¼ cup olive oil
2 Tbsp. basil, powdered
½ cup chopped walnuts

1 tsp. prepared mustard
Pinch of stevia powder or 1 tsp.
honey

Blend all in a blender and use it to dress a salad of spinach, grated carrots, lamb's quarters and sprouts.

—MAIA BALLIS, REPRINTED WITH PERMISSION FROM
SUN MOUNTAIN NATURAL FOODS COOKBOOK

Nettle Vinegar

Harvest nettle plants before they produce their lacy flowers. (Using rubber gloves will protect you from their sting.) Wash and fill a small jar to the top with the fresh nettle. Pour apple cider vinegar to the top. Place a piece of plastic wrap over the top of the jar and put a lid on over the plastic. You don't need the plastic if your jar lid is sealed with one of the food-grade sealants so that it resists the rusting action of vinegar. Let steep for 2–4 weeks. Strain and use over salads.

NETTLE SALAD DRESSING

⅔ cup nettle vinegar
⅓ cup ume plum vinegar
½ cup olive oil

Pour ingredients in a salad dressing bottle. Shake before using. Store in the refrigerator. Makes 1½ cups.

—Risa Mornis

SOUPS

A soup offers so much and requires so little, two reasons why it is a favorite form of food. A nourishing soup can take on many flavors, textures and aromas and offers an emotional appeal, too. For herbalists, soup is a favorite for many reasons: It is a highly nutritious way to consume healing foods and herbs, it warms the body and it tastes good. The warming quality of soup (clear soup in particular) is identical to that of tea and is often the vehicle the body needs for ridding itself of colds, influenzas and infections. To an herbalist, a soup is actually a kind of savory tea. It can be food and medicine at the same time. The recipes here reflect our desire to take our medicine in as nourishing and tasty a manner as possible.

DANDELION GREEN SOUP

As a first course or as a meal in itself, this soup is sure to stimulate the body's digestive juices while pleasing the palate. Other bitter greens can be added or substituted if fresh dandelion greens are not in season.

1 lb. fresh dandelion greens	6 cups of water
2 large carrots	¼ cup miso paste
1 oz. fresh ginger root	2 Tbsp. apple cider vinegar (or
2 cloves raw garlic	more to taste)

Rinse the greens thoroughly and chop into bite-sized pieces along with carrots. Peel and slice ginger and garlic into chunks. Steam all together for five minutes or until carrots are tender. Place steamed veggies in a food processor and purée, adding small amounts of water as needed to make smooth. Heat water in a saucepan at a medium high heat but do not boil. Stir in miso paste until dissolved; then add puréed vegetables and vinegar. Mix well and serve warm with croutons, mini rice cakes or a sprinkling of sesame seeds on top. Serves 4–6 people.

—ANDREA MURRAY

Wild Seasonings

Wild seasonings bring a unique dimension to cooking; however, many wild plants lose flavor when dried or exposed to heat. Here are a few that stand up to cultivated herbs.

- **Queen Anne's lace** leaves may be used as parsley.

- **Yarrow** leaves or buds have a mellow sage-like flavor.

- **Wild ginger, spicebush** or **sassafras** may be used whenever cinnamon or allspice is called for.

- **Sweet cicely** has a light anise flavor.

- **Sorrel** and **smartweed** add a slight lemony flavor.

- **Sweetgale** imparts a mild sage/bay flavor.

- **Sweetfern** leaves are a cross between mace and bay.

- **Wild leeks** are more pungent than onions.

- **Black birch** twigs are a source of wintergreen flavor that will hold up to storage and heat.

- **Yellow sweet clover** has a sweet vanilla-like flavor.

—JOYCE WARDWELL

CHILLED SAGE BLOSSOM
AND CUCUMBER SOUP

Great on a hot summer night. Delicious and easy.

4 cups chopped cucumber
  (about 2 large cucumbers)
2 cups water
½ cup of fresh sage blossoms

1 Tbsp. honey
2 cups yogurt
2 Tbsp. fresh parsley

Peel the cucumber, remove the seeds and chop into pieces. Add the cucumber, water and sage blossoms to a blender and purée until smooth. Transfer to a bowl, and add the honey, yogurt and parsley. Mix well and chill at least ½ hour before serving. Garnish with sage blossoms. Serves 4–5.

—RACHEL SCHNEIDER, FLOWER POWER HERBALS

SORREL SOUP

2 cups chopped garden sorrel
1 small onion, chopped
2 cloves garlic, chopped
2 medium potatoes, chopped

2 pints stock
1 Tbsp. butter
Nutmeg to taste
Yogurt for garnish

Steam sorrel lightly and sauté with garlic, onions, butter and nutmeg. Add the potatoes and stock and cook until potatoes are soft. Purée in blender. Serve topped with yogurt. The sorrel can be substituted with lovage, nettles, spinach or chard. Serves 3–4.

—MARY BOVE

Sheep Sorrel
(*Rumex acetosella*)

Full of flavor and vitamins, the wild sheep sorrel imparts its own distinct lemony sour taste to many dishes and can be used instead of garden sorrel in sorrel soup. If the sourness is too much for you, cut it by substituting some spinach, lamb's quarters or lettuce for some of the sorrel. Sheep sorrel's traditional uses are as a diuretic and refrigerant—excellent for cooling fevers and inflammation. Sheep sorrel is also a main ingredient in the folk cancer remedy called Essiac.

IMMUNE-BOOSTING ROOTS
& HERBS POTAGE

1–2 fresh burdock roots, chopped
2–3 fresh dandelion roots, chopped
3 handfuls dried nettles, crushed
2½ quarts nonchlorinated water
8–9 fresh or dried shiitake mushrooms, chopped
1 medium onion, chopped
5–6 grams kelp, crushed
1 cup whole grain basmati or brown rice
¼ cup tamari
¼ cup apple cider vinegar
2 Tbsp. miso
6–8 cloves garlic, chopped

Cover burdock and dandelion roots with water. Cook 15–20 minutes over medium heat or until tender. You can pour off this water to make the soup less bitter, adding 2½ cups fresh water. However, you will be pouring out nutrients as well, so you might want to retain this nutrient-rich water and enjoy the bitter taste. Add remaining ingredients with the exception of miso and garlic. Cover and bring to a boil. Reduce heat and simmer 1½ hours. Add miso and garlic right before serving. This soup has an exceptional taste that improves with age and is strengthening to the immune system and all our systems and cells. For variety, try adding beans, cabbage, carrots, beets and other root vegetables. 8–10 servings.

—SUZANNE NAGLER

Roots in Soups

For extra-delicious flavor, always roast any root veggies with olive oil until brown. Then add to soup.

—BRYAN RAY KEITH

Salt Substitute

3 parts marjoram
2 parts parsley
2 parts basil

1 part thyme
1 part crushed rosemary
½ part minced onion (dried)

Mix well. Store in glass jar. Use as desired in any dish. Make sure the rosemary leaves are well crushed to avoid their sharp edges.

—Kathleen Duffy

WILD THING SOUP

1 Tbsp. olive oil
1 medium onion, chopped fine
1 clove garlic, chopped
2 tsp. curry powder
2 cups chopped potato

4 cups mixed wild greens,
    washed and chopped, such as
    violet, nettle, malva and
    lamb's quarters
4 cups water
½ tsp. salt
pepper and tamari to taste

In a soup pot, sauté the onions, garlic and curry powder in olive oil, stirring constantly. Add the potatoes and wild greens. Sauté briefly. Then add the water. Cook until the potatoes are tender. Cool for a short while and then blend the ingredients in a blender. Return to the soup pot to reheat and season with salt, pepper and tamari. Serves 3–4.

—Brigitte Mars

Substitutes for Wild Greens

Expert substituting calls for knowledge of the taste of wild greens. Lacking this, the categories below can help you choose your greens.

MILD FLAVORS

Wild: Amaranth, chickweed, lamb's quarters, mallow, nettle, violets and purslane.

Garden/supermarket greens: Kale, romaine, green lettuces, bok choy, cabbages, spinach, Swiss chard.

SOUR FLAVORS

Wild: Sheep sorrel, yellow dock, wood sorrel.

Garden/supermarket greens: Garden sorrel, spinach, cabbages.

BITTER FLAVORS

Wild: Dandelion, yellow dock, plantains.

Garden/supermarket greens: Dandelion, chicory.

HOT/SPICY FLAVORS

Wild: Watercress, mustards.

Garden/supermarket greens: Watercress, mustards, arugula.

NETTLE LENTIL SOUP

1 cup lentils, soaked overnight
1 bay leaf
5 cups water
3 Tbsp. olive oil
1 large red or yellow onion, or 2
  leeks, chopped
2 medium potatoes, cubed

4 cloves garlic
3 Tbsp. fresh parsley, chopped
½ cup chopped and steamed
  nettles
½ tsp. thyme
Pinch of cayenne
2 Tbsp. miso
3 medium tomatoes, fresh or
  canned

Put the presoaked drained lentils and bay leaf in a soup pot with the water. Bring to a boil and scoop off any foam that forms, then lower the heat to a slow boil for 30 minutes. While the lentils are cooking, heat the oil in a skillet and lightly sauté onion, potatoes, garlic and thyme. Combine the lentils with the onion and potato mixture and cook another 20–30 minutes. When the lentils are soft, stir in the chopped parsley, nettles, cayenne, tomatoes and miso. Thin the soup with water if necessary. Serves 4–6. This soup would be nicely complemented with dumplings. (Recipe follows.)

—Jo Jenner

Beans & Greens

When cooking any kind of dried beans always add lots of steamed greens of any kind. They bring out each other's flavors in a delicious, nutritious way.

—Brian Ray Keith

FLAX DUMPLINGS

Grind 1 cup flaxseed. Add 1 cup vegetable broth. Allow to sit till thick. Pinch off small balls and cook in clear soup. These are pleasant and satisfying. See page 202 for more about flax.

—CATHY GILEADI-SWEET

NETTLE DUMPLINGS

½ cup nettles, steamed and chopped
1½ cups pastry flour
1 Tbsp. baking powder
½ tsp. salt
1 egg

½ cup water or rice, nut or soy milk
1 tsp. oil
1 tsp. vinegar
2 cloves garlic, minced

Steam enough nettle tops to make ½ cup chopped. Mix together flour, baking powder and salt. Beat the egg in a measuring cup and add enough water or rice milk to make ¾ cup of liquid. Add chopped nettles, oil, vinegar and garlic to the egg mixture. Lightly stir the liquid ingredients into the flour. Bring broth or soup to a boil in a large pot. Drop heaping tablespoons of the dumpling mixture into the water. Cook for 10 minutes, turning the dumplings in the water after 5 minutes. Scoop out of broth and serve immediately with soup or stew. Makes 36–40 1-inch dumplings.

—JO JENNER

BARLEY VEGETABLE SOUP

1 cup chopped onion
2–3 cloves garlic
4 oz. shiitake mushrooms
2 stalks celery, chopped
2 carrots, chopped
1 cup TVP (soy grits)
2 Tbsp. olive oil
3 quarts water

1 cup barley
Dulse
Salt and pepper to taste
1–2 cups chopped winter squash
2 Tbsp. miso
Herbs to flavor (rosemary,
    thyme, oregano or basil)

Sauté onions, garlic, mushrooms, celery, carrots and TVP in olive oil until soft. Add 3 quarts of water and the barley. Add dulse, salt and pepper to taste. Simmer covered for 2–3 hours. Add squash, miso and herbs ½ hour before serving. Add more water if needed. Serve hot with warm whole grain bread or rolls. Serves 12.

—Jane Smolnik

MEXICAN SPICE SOUP

1 onion
1 head garlic
4 stalks celery
1 green pepper
2 tomatoes
2 Tbsp. olive oil
1 tsp. dried basil (or 1 Tbsp fresh)

¼ cup chopped fresh parsley
1 tsp. cumin
Dried or fresh hot pepper to
    taste
Salt to taste
Water

Chop veggies. Sauté onion and garlic until soft. Add celery, pepper, herbs and spices and sauté briefly. Add enough water to make a thin broth and simmer one hour. Add chopped tomato. Serve over corn chips and grated cheese of your choice. Serves 4–8.

—Jane Dwinell

GARLIC SOUP

This garlic soup is reserved for special occasions in our house. It appears when poor winter-weary bodies need a dose of something good for us. It is especially good if you've come down with a cold or the flu. It's the herb garden equivalent of chicken soup, good for you and good for the soul.

2 quarts water
1 whole head of garlic, cloves
   separated but unpeeled
1 tsp. salt and a pinch of pepper,
   if desired

Lots of fresh herbs including
   parsley, sage, fennel, rosemary
   (a 2-inch sprig), thyme,
   chives, etc.
2 egg yolks
3 Tbsp. olive oil

Place all ingredients except the egg yolks and oil in a sauce pan, bring to a boil, then simmer gently for 30 minutes. Strain out the solids and return the soup to the pan. Beat the egg yolks with a whisk, then beat the olive oil into them. Whisk a small amount of the hot soup into the egg yolk mixture, then another ladleful. Add the egg-soup blend back into the soup, stirring as you go. Serve immediately. Serves 8.

—DELL RATCLIFFE, *COUNTRY SHEPHERD HERB NEWS*

Growing Garlic

Fall is the time of year to plant garlic. Simply buy large whole heads of garlic from the grocery store and separate the cloves. Plant individual cloves 6-inches apart in fertile garden soil along the edge of your vegetable garden or tucked into empty areas of your herb garden. The garlic cloves will sprout and grow over the winter. Plant plenty, the green shoots can be used for flavoring, similar to green onions. The garlic will grow strong and green next spring and be ready to harvest in early to mid-summer when the leaves yellow. Dig carefully and allow to dry for long-term storage.

—DELL RATCLIFFE, *COUNTRY SHEPHERD HERB NEWS*

STRONG BONE STEW

Thirteen great calcium-rich foods all in one pot.

2 Tbsp. olive oil
1 cup organic onions, chopped
1–3 cloves garlic, chopped
1 cup quartered mushrooms
1 quart vegetable stock or water
1 cup each of at least four of
  these organically-grown vegetables, cubed, unpeeled:
  sweet potato, carrot, turnip,
  winter squash, potato,
  parsnip, burdock/gobo

½ cup dried wakame seaweed,
  cut small
2 Tbsp. miso
2 tsp. tamari
⅓ cup tahini
2 Tbsp. peanut or almond butter
1 Tbsp. cronewort vinegar (see
  next page)
1 cake tofu, cubed

In a large, heavy-bottomed pot, heat the olive oil and sauté the onions, garlic and mushrooms. When the onions are soft, add the vegetable stock or water and bring to a boil. Add the vegetables and seaweed. Simmer for 45 minutes, adding more water or broth if needed. While the stew simmers, mix the miso, tamari, tahini, peanut or almond butter and vinegar together in a large measuring cup or bowl. Just before serving, ladle enough hot broth into the measuring cup or bowl to make a mixture thin enough to pour into the stew. Add this mix and the tofu to your stewpot. Continue to cook on very low heat for 5 minutes. Serve hot with whole grain bread or brown rice. Serves 3–4.

—Susun Weed, reprinted with permission from *Menopausal Years,*
The Wise Woman Way

Cronewort Vinegar

Cronewort (*Artemisia vulgaris,* usually called mugwort) is especially rich in calcium, and vinegars are especially effective mediums for extracting the mineral richness of plants.

Fill a jar to the top with freshly gathered mugwort leaves and stems. Fill with vinegar (apple cider vinegar, wine vinegar or rice vinegar are the best choices; do not use white vinegar), label and cap. Vinegar can corrode metal, so use plastic lids or corks or put a piece of plastic wrap over the jar before screwing on a metal lid. Let steep for 3–6 weeks, and strain. Add this calcium-rich vinegar to your salads, steamed vegetables and other recipes whenever vinegar is called for.

CHICKEN AND NOODLE SOUP

1 Tbsp. sesame oil
2 Tbsp. soy sauce
2 tsp. grated fresh ginger
1 cup chopped raw chicken
Green vegetables, thinly sliced
1 liter of good chicken stock
2 sprigs mint
6-inch long piece lemon grass

Handful of instant noodles
2 tsp. sugar
2 tsp. herb vinegar (I use a rice vinegar infused with garlic, ginger, lemon grass and coriander seeds.)
2–3 spring onions for garnish

In a heavy pan heat sesame oil, soy sauce and ginger; add chicken and sauté over high heat. Add vegetables and stock, mint and lemon grass. Bring to a boil and cook 2 minutes. Add noodles, sugar and vinegar. When the noodles are cooked, remove the mint and lemon grass, place in serving bowls and garnish with spring onions. Serves 4.

—JANE CARDEN

Scarborough Fair Seasoning

This classic blend is easy to make and can be added to soups, stews, sautéed vegetables, etc. Place herb blend in a clean glass jar, label and decorate with a sprig of fresh rosemary. Include a recipe (such as Herb Roasted Nuts, page 23) that features this blend. Use only high-quality organic herbs. Makes a great gift for beginning herb cooks.

½ cup dried parsley
¼ cup dried sage
¼ cup dried thyme
¼ cup dried rosemary

Remove any stems and crumble the parsley, sage and thyme into small pieces. Grind the rosemary to a medium texture in a mortar and pestle or coffee grinder that is used only for herbs. Blend all the ingredients and store in a glass jar away from heat, moisture and light for up to one year. Makes 1¼ cups.

—Sharleen Andrews-Miller

CREAMY SQUASH SOUP

¼ tsp. rosemary
¼ tsp. marjoram
2 Tbsp. butter

1 cup cooked, mashed squash
2 cups milk
½ cup half-and-half

Sauté rosemary and marjoram in butter. Add cooked squash and sauté until soft. Gradually add milk and stir to a simmer. Add half-and-half and serve. Serves 2.

—Mary Ellen Ross

Herb Hint

Crush the herb in the palm of your hand with the heel of your other hand before adding it to the pot to release its full flavor.

CARROT CHIVE SOUP

1 head garlic
1 large Spanish or sweet onion
2 Tbsp. butter
2 Tbsp. olive oil
1 lb. carrots
1 tsp. dried dillweed (or 1 Tbsp. fresh)

½ cup or more chopped fresh chives
Water
Salt and pepper to taste

Chop garlic and onion. Melt butter and olive oil in heavy soup pot. Sauté garlic and onion until clear and soft. Add chopped carrots. Continue to sauté vegetables until carrots are nicely browned and soft, stirring frequently over medium heat. Add dill and water to cover. Cook another hour. Add more water if necessary. You may blend this soup in blender or food processor or eat as is. Serve with fresh chives, as many as you like. Serves 8–10.

—JANE DWINELL

DANDELION MATZO BALL SOUP

2 Tbsp. melted chicken fat (or oil)
2 eggs, slightly beaten
1½ cups matzo meal
1 Tbsp. salt
2 Tbsp. chicken broth
3 quarts chicken broth

¼ cup diced carrots
¼ cup fresh onions, chopped
1 cup fresh dandelion leaves, chopped
Croutons and additional chopped dandelion leaves

Blend fat or oil with eggs. Add to matzo meal and salt. Blend well. Then add the 2 Tbsp. broth. Mix until uniform. Refrigerate for 15 minutes. Bring 3 quarts chicken broth, carrots, onions and 1 cup dandelion leaves to a boil. Make matzo batter into balls by dropping teaspoonsful into the soup. Turn heat down to a gentle boil for 30–40 minutes. Garnish finished soup with croutons and a little chopped fresh dandelion. You can also add ¼ cup dandelion leaves to the matzo meal mixture. Serves 6–8.

—PETER GAIL, REPRINTED WITH PERMISSION
FROM *THE GREAT DANDELION COOKBOOK*.

FRESH TOMATO BASIL SOUP

1 onion, chopped
Several cloves garlic, chopped
2 Tbsp. butter or olive oil
2 lb. fresh tomatoes, chopped
½ cup chopped fresh basil, plus additional for garnish

2 Tbsp. honey or maple syrup
¼ cup brandy (optional)
Water to cover
Salt and pepper to taste

Sauté onion and garlic in butter or olive oil until soft. Add rest of ingredients. Cook on low heat for 1–2 hours. May be blended or served as is. Good hot or cold. Garnish with fresh basil. Serves 5–8.

—JANE DWINELL

When You Don't Have Fresh Herbs

Reduce the amount of herb used by two-thirds when substituting dried herbs for fresh in cooking.

NAVY BEAN AND VEGETABLE SOUP

16 oz. package navy beans
4 red potatoes
2 carrots
2 leeks
3 garlic cloves, minced
¼ onion

1 bay leaf
2 tsp. dried angelica leaves
1 tsp. dried wild oregano leaves
1 tsp. dried cicely leaves
2 tsp. Spike

Soak beans overnight. Strain the next day and sort through for imperfect beans. Chop vegetables into bite-sized pieces. Place beans and vegetables into 6 cups of water. Mix in dried spices. Simmer in crock pot all day or until beans and vegetables are tender. Serve with crackers. Yields at least 10 bowls of soup.

—FEATHER JONES, ROCKY MOUNTAIN CENTER FOR BOTANICAL STUDIES

SAUCES

ROASTED GARLIC
AND RED CHILE PEPPER PURÉE

1 cup peeled garlic cloves
¼ cup olive oil
3–4 red jalapenos (if you want the purée hot)
8–12 red roasting peppers (Nu Mex chiles or pablanos are good)
Salt to taste

Lightly brown peeled garlic cloves in a heavy pan with olive oil. Roast all peppers over an open flame or under the broiler until soft. Cool. Peel chili peppers and remove the seeds. Process all ingredients in a food processor. Use as a sauce or dip. It is great on crab cakes. Use green chilies if you want a green sauce. Makes about ½ cup.

—JILL YECK, PECONIC RIVER HERB FARM

GINGER-GARLIC SESAME SAUCE

Don't let the large amount of garlic in this recipe scare you off! This wonderfully spicy sauce has helped our family through many seasons of colds and flu. Great on steamed or sautéed vegetables, pasta and grain dishes.

10–13 cloves organic garlic
¼ cup tamari or shoyu soy sauce
½ cup sesame butter (tahini)
1-inch piece ginger root, grated
4 tsp. dark toasted sesame oil

Juice of 1 organic lemon
Grated lemon peel to taste
Water (to thin to gravy consistency)
Honey to taste

Blend all ingredients in a food processor or blender. (It will be thick.) Drizzle water in as you blend until the mixture reaches gravy consistency. Add honey to taste, to mellow flavors. Serve over cooked vegetables, pasta, grain dishes and entrées. Makes 1–2 cups.

—GAIL ULRICH, BLAZING STAR HERBAL SCHOOL

Ginger

The taste of ginger is loved by people around the world and is one of the most widely cultivated spices. It is well-known for both its edible and medicinal values. Medicinally it has been used for everything from morning sickness and migraines to colds and fevers. Because of its availability, it is one of the first herbs that people try when considering herbal medicine. Fresh ginger root is the preferred form for medicinal use. It can be made into a tea or applied externally by compress. To make a tea, place ½ teaspoon of freshly chopped or grated ginger into 8 ounces of boiling water, cover pot and steep for 10–15 minutes. Strain and add honey to taste.

CHUTNEY

2 oz. mint leaves
4 oz. onion
Green or red pepper to taste

Salt to taste
4 oz. unripe mango or kiwi fruit
 pulp

Mix all ingredients in a blender to form a thick paste.

—Dr. H. S. Puri

CHILI-BASIL SAUCE

Because of their stimulating effects, red chili peppers have become a common synergist for herbal formulas and ethnic cooking. Complementing the chili peppers' strong actions are the soothing properties of basil leaf, making every dish touched by this sauce a fantastic gastrointestinal experience.

1 cup dried red chili peppers, large or small
2 cups water
2 cups fresh basil, or ¾ cup dried

2 cloves fresh garlic
2 Tbsp. tamari or soy sauce
Juice of 1 lemon

Pull stems off peppers, rinse and place in saucepan with water. Bring to a boil and let simmer for 20 minutes with lid on. Strain peppers and save the water. Place peppers, basil and garlic in a food processor and purée. Add a small amount of saved water, if needed, to make a paste out of ingredients. The paste can be very spicy, depending upon the peppers. Start with ¼ cup of paste in a bowl and whip in tamari, lemon juice and enough water to make a pourable sauce. Add more paste to sauce as needed to satisfy palate. The sauce makes an excellent condiment for Sea Vegeta-balls (page 121), stir-fries, whole grains and potatoes. The paste can be added directly to bean dishes and soups as a spicy stock and can be stored in the refrigerator for several weeks. Makes about 3 cups.

—Andrea Murray

Herb Hint

When you are experimenting with an unfamiliar herb, remember that it is far easier to add more later than to take it out.

JOY'S MUSHROOM SAGE SAUCE

This mild white sauce tastes delicious on meat or fish.

½ red onion, sliced thinly
5–6 mushrooms, chopped fine
1 cup milk

Dab of sour cream or butter
1–2 Tbsp. sifted flour
Dried sage leaves to taste

Sauté sliced onions and mushrooms. As the mushrooms soften slowly add milk, sour cream or butter and sifted flour, stirring until thickened and smooth. Stir in the sage leaves, powdering them between your fingers as you put them into the sauce. Simmer and stir for a few more minutes. Serve over meat, fish or vegetable dishes. Makes 1 cup.

—RISA MORNIS

RHUBARB AND GINGER REMOULADE

2½ cups celery, diced
1½ scallions, diced
2 stalks rhubarb, sliced
3 Tbsp. hot mustard
1½ tsp. salt
½ tsp. freshly ground black pepper
1 Tbsp. paprika
½ tsp. sweet cicely leaves (or ¼ teaspoon ground fennel seed)

1 Tbsp. finely diced fresh ginger root
¼ tsp. red pepper
1½ Tbsp. lemon juice
1 Tbsp. sugar
¾ cup red wine vinegar
1 cup canola oil (do not use olive oil)
¼ cup wild leeks, sliced

Put the diced celery and scallions into a 2½ quart container. Reserve. Cook the sliced stalks of rhubarb in as little water as possible until soft, but not mushy and set aside. Put the rest of the ingredients in a blender (except the oil and leeks) and blend on low speed. Slowly add most of the oil. Add the rhubarb stalks and leeks, top with the rest of the oil and blend until smooth.

Taste and adjust seasonings. You may want to add more sugar. Pour the mixture over the chopped celery and scallions and mix together well. Let rest for 6 hours or more before using to give the flavors a chance to blend together.

Remoulade is excellent as a sauce for cold seafoods, grilled meats, sandwich spreads and grilled vegetables. Makes 3–4 cups.

—JOYCE WARDWELL

Sweet Sauces

FENNEL LIME SAUCE

Fennel grows wild in so many places and flowers twice a year in California. Try this sauce made of the zippy green seed. It has a refreshing tingle that will clear your palate, freshen your breath and help your digestion. I've used it on baked apples with a sprig of fennel flowers in the center of the bowl.

¼ cup honey
¼ cup fresh green fennel seeds, ground
2 Tbsp. lime juice
⅓ fennel head or mint leaves for garnish

Grind ingredients together and let sit for a day to draw out flavors. Marinate apple chunks in it or add it to baked apples. It takes about two heads of fennel to obtain ¼ cup of seed. Use ⅓ head to garnish the center of your serving bowl or tuck mint around the edges. Yields ½ cup.

—Maia Ballis, reprinted with permission from
Sun Mountain Natural Foods Cookbook

Fennel

Early herbalists used this herb to make fat people thin and improve eyesight. I don't know about the first use, but the second is valid and still in use. Fennel's main use now is as a digestive aid, relieving flatulence and colic. It is also an antispasmodic used to relieve bronchitis and coughs. Because of its sweet flavor, it makes a nice cough syrup. To make a tea of fennel seeds, bruise 1 teaspoon of seeds in a mortar and pestle and pour a cup of boiling water over them. Steep for 5 minutes and strain.

ROSEMARY SPICED PEAR SAUCE

1 cup white wine vinegar
1 cup water
1 cup white sugar
2 dried chilies

4 sprigs fresh rosemary, stems removed
4 peeled, quartered and cored pears

Put all the ingredients in a saucepan and boil until the sugar has dissolved. Turn down the heat and simmer until tender. Cool and store in the refrigerator for a month to develop flavor. Serve with ham or cold meat or add to a cheese board. Yields 2–3 cups.

—Jane Carden

ROSE HIP SAUCE

2 cups water
1 cup sugar
2 cups fresh picked rosehips

Put water and sugar in a pan and boil until the sugar has melted. Slice rosehips in half and add to sugar mixture, cooking gently for 1 hour. Strain through a sieve and cool. Yields 2–3 cups.

—Mary Bove

Rose Hips

Rose hips are one of the best sources of vitamin C and can be used for fighting colds and other infections, such as sore throats and influenza. Rose hip syrup is an easy way to administer medicine to children who won't or can't take their vitamin C. Rose hips are commonly made into jams and jellies, and rose hip sauce can be added to many dessert dishes.

WILD BERRY SAUCE

Most wild berries must first be run through a ricer and a strainer to remove seeds. You may wish to de-seed a small amount of berries by hand to add for texture.

    2 cups berry purée (try wintergreen, rosehips, hawthorn,
        chokecherry, mountain ash)
    1 Tbsp. cornstarch
    2 Tbsp. kirsch or other fruit brandy

Bring the berry purée to a boil. Dissolve cornstarch in the liquor. Add to the berries. Immediately reduce heat to low. Stir constantly while mixture thickens. Remove from heat and cool. Makes about 2 cups.

—JOYCE WARDWELL

BREADS & BUTTERS

OLIVE BASIL MUFFINS
WITH PARMESAN TOPPING

2 cups flour
1 Tbsp. baking powder
1 Tbsp. sugar
1 egg
⅔ cup milk
1 Tbsp. olive oil
½ cup butter, melted
¼ cup pitted chopped olives
¼ cup chopped anchovies

¼ cup fresh chopped basil
3 spring onions, chopped
1 clove crushed garlic
1 Tbsp. chopped fresh oregano

Parmesan Topping
¾ cup fresh bread crumbs
½ cup fresh grated Parmesan
3 Tbsp. melted butter

Mix flour, baking powder and sugar. Whisk together the egg, milk, oil and butter. Pour into the dry ingredients. Add the next six ingredients. Spoon into greased muffin tins ⅔ full. Combine the topping ingredients and sprinkle on muffins. Bake at 400° F for 15–20 minutes. Makes 12 muffins.

—JANE CARDIN

Mallow

Mallow (*Malva sylvestris* or *neglecta*) is a common roadside plant with edible and medicinal properties. Both the leaves and the flower petals are edible. Medicinally, mallow has been used as a demulcent for respiratory and digestive ailments such as bronchitis, laryngitis, stomach ulcers and gastritis. Externally, it is helpful for soothing skin irritations, burns and insect bites. "We harvest the leaves and dry them. Then we grind them into a powder by placing them in a pillowcase (or equivalent), closing it tightly and rubbing it till the leaves are reduced to a powder."

—Peter Bigfoot

GREEN CORN BREAD

This corn bread comes out a bright golden green! It is a richly nutritious bread, nearly a meal in itself.

1½ cups yellow corn meal	2 cups rice milk
½ cup whole wheat flour	1 Tbsp. maple syrup
1 cup mallow leaf flour	½ cup corn oil
1 cup mesquite bean pod flour*	6 eggs
⅛ cup baking powder	2 crushed dried jalapeno peppers

Preheat oven to 375° F. Grease a 9 x 14 inch bread pan and sprinkle it with flour. Mix the dry ingredients together. In a separate bowl mix wet ingredients with an egg beater. Whisk the wet and dry ingredients together, add crushed peppers and pour into the pan. Bake until done, about 25 minutes.

—Peter Bigfoot, Reevis Mountain School of Self-reliance

*See page 105

Mesquite Bean Pod Flour

The mesquite is a wild bean tree that grows in the southwest U.S. Its beans mature in July. The ripe bean pods turn a light yellow-brown color, and are dry to the touch. The thickened pods contain and yield a sugary sweet powder when crushed in a grinder or a strong blender. The bean pods were once the most important staple food of the Native Americans of this region. They are very nutritious. The actual bean seed is usually discarded. Like carob, it is the pod that is used.

—PETER BIGFOOT

MORNING BISCUITS WITH ROSEMARY

These biscuits can be served with soup or salad or spread with jam or cream cheese at teatime.

1 cup unbleached white flour	2 Tbsp. butter
1 cup whole wheat flour	¾ cup milk
1 tsp. baking powder	2 tsp. crumbled, dried rosemary
½ tsp. baking soda	(or 2 Tbsp. fresh, chopped
Dash of salt	fine)
½ Tbsp. sugar	

Sift the flours, baking powder, baking soda, salt and sugar together in a large bowl. With a fork or pastry cutter, work the butter into the dry ingredients. Some small lumps will remain. Add the milk and rosemary and mix well to form a soft dough. Roll out the dough to ½-inch thickness on a lightly floured surface. Cut into 2-inch rounds and place on a greased and lightly floured baking sheet. Bake for 20 minutes in a preheated 400° F oven. Makes about 1½ dozen biscuits.

—KARYN SIEGAL-MAIER

Biscuit Tip

The secret to good biscuits is to cut straight down with the cutter and not make any twists or turns with it. Use a cutter that is 1½–3 inches in diameter and height. Cut as many biscuits as your cutter size will allow, and then gently reroll the dough once more. Repeat cutting until all dough is used. Place the biscuits so that their sides touch on an ungreased baking sheet.

—Karyn Siegal-Maier

Calendula Biscuits

1⅓ cups unbleached white flour
⅔ cup whole wheat flour
2 tsp. baking powder
½ tsp. baking soda

⅓ cup calendula petals, washed and chopped
⅓ cup canola or other vegetable oil
½ cup pineapple juice

Combine the flours, baking powder, baking soda and calendula petals in a large bowl, but do not stir. Make a "tunnel" in the center of the flour mixture and slowly pour in the oil and pineapple juice. Stir with a fork just until blended. The dough should just pull away from the side of the bowl. Add more liquid if necessary to achieve this texture. Turn dough out onto a lightly floured surface. Roll out gently to a thickness of ½ inch. Cut into 2-inch rounds and place the biscuits so that their sides touch on an ungreased baking sheet. Bake for 10–12 minutes in a preheated 450° F oven. Serve hot with an herbal butter or jam. Makes about 20 biscuits.

—Karyn Siegal Maier

DILL AND POTATO CAKES

2 cups self-rising flour
3 Tbsp. butter, softened
Pinch of salt
1 Tbsp. finely chopped fresh dill

1 cup mashed potatoes, freshly made
2–3 Tbsp. milk, as required

Preheat the oven to 450° F. Sift the flour into a bowl and add the butter, salt and dill. Mix in the mashed potatoes and enough milk to make a soft, pliable dough. Roll the dough out on a well-floured surface until it is fairly thin. Cut into several neat rounds with a 3-inch cutter. Grease a cookie sheet, place the cakes on it, and bake for 20–25 minutes until golden. Makes about 15 biscuits.

—FEATHER JONES, ROCKY MOUNTAIN CENTER FOR BOTANICAL STUDIES

SWISS CHEESE LOAF

1 Tbsp. yeast
½ cup hot tap water
½ cup maple syrup
1 tsp. salt (optional)
½ cup vegetable oil

3 eggs
1 cup Swiss cheese
¼ cup fresh chives
¼ cup fresh lovage
2 cups flour

Combine all ingredients and knead well. Place in a warm oven (250° F) and let rise. Bake at 375° F for 30 minutes. Remove and cool on rack.

—JAN SHIMP

GRANDMA MORNIS' 3-HERB BREAD

1½ tsp. dry yeast
1½ Tbsp. sugar
3 cups bread flour
1 tsp. salt
7 oz. warm water

2 oz. warm milk
1½ Tbsp. butter
3 Tbsp. crushed dried chives
3 Tbsp. crushed dried dill
1 Tbsp. crushed dried parsley

Mix all ingredients. Add more flour if needed. Fold dough over and press with heel of your hand, turn and fold again. Repeat, kneading dough until it is smooth, elastic and satiny—about 10–15 minutes. Add extra flour if needed. Place dough in a large greased bowl and turn to coat. Cover with a dish towel and let it rise in a warm draft-free place (75–85 degrees). When the dough has doubled in 1–2 hours, punch it down. Press it out, fold it toward its center and shape into a loaf. Cover again with a cloth and leave it to rise until almost doubled in bulk. Preheat oven to 350° F. Bake for 35–45 minutes. This recipe can also be used in a bread machine.

—RISA MORNIS

ITALIAN HERB BREAD

This food processor recipe appears long but it is very easy to make and tastes wonderful!

¼ cup warm water (not too hot—test on your wrist)

1 package active dry yeast plus 1 teaspoon of sugar

1 Tbsp. sugar

3 to 3½ cups unbleached flour, preferably organic bread flour. (The extra ½ cup may be necessary when there is a high amount of humidity in the air.)

1 tsp. salt

1 Tbsp. fresh thyme leaves

¼ cup fresh sage leaves

1 tsp. crushed fresh rosemary leaves

2 Tbsp. extra virgin olive oil

¼ cup warm milk (nonfat or regular)

3 Tbsp. grated Parmesan cheese

Add ¼ cup warm water to the food processor (with blade attachment). Sprinkle the yeast and 1 teaspoon of the sugar over water and let stand until yeast starts to grow. Add 3 cups of the flour plus the salt, remaining sugar, herbs and olive oil to processor and pulse to mix well, about 15 seconds. (The yeast will remain on the bottom until liquid is added.) Slowly add warm milk while running processor. Process for 40–60 seconds or until dough pulls away from the side. Test dough (Flour your hands and take a small piece of dough out and stretch it. It should be a silky smooth consistency; if it is grainy-looking, continue to process). If the dough is too wet, add the remaining flour a little at a time. If it is too dry, add very little water while running processor. Test again. The dough should come out of the processor in one piece and be elastic. Do not knead the dough.

Put the dough in a large bowl and cover with plastic wrap. Let rise in a warm place without drafts until doubled (about 1–1½ hours). Punch down and roll out on a floured surface. Roll out to the length of a baking sheet and put dough on sheet. Sprinkle Parmesan cheese on rolled-out dough. Roll up and pinch the seam tightly and pinch the ends so the cheese does not come out during baking. Cover with a towel and let double in size again. Just before putting in oven, mist with a fine spray of water. Cook in a preheated oven at 375° F. for 20–25 minutes. The loaf should sound hollow when tapped on the bottom. Let cool for 30 minutes on a cooling rack before cutting.

—JO-ANN ALBANO, LADYBUG KNOLL

COTTAGE HERB BREAD

This bread is styled after an Irish soda bread recipe. It is quick and versatile. Use whatever herb you have the most of.

¾ cup cottage cheese
¾ cup milk
2 eggs
½ cup fresh parsley
¼ cup one fresh herb or a blend
   (try thyme, rosemary, sage,
   summer savory, basil)

3 cups flour (½ white, ½ whole
   wheat)
1 tsp. salt
2 tsp. baking powder
⅓ cup soft butter

Preheat oven to 350° F. Butter a round baking dish. Put cottage cheese, milk, eggs and all fresh herbs in a blender. Blend at medium speed until smooth. In a large bowl mix the flour, salt and baking powder. Cut in butter until it is crumbly. Stir cottage cheese-herb mix into the flour mix until well blended. Dough should be firm enough to mound in the baking dish. Smooth the top with wet hands. Sprinkle with chopped rosemary and bake 45–60 minutes. Enjoy warm.

—LINDA QUINTANA

JUDI'S DANDYLION PIZZA BREAD

3 to 3½ cups all-purpose flour
1 packet quick-rising yeast
2 Tbsp. oil
1 Tbsp. sugar
2 tsp. salt
1 cup hot water
Cornmeal
Fresh or dried rosemary,
   snipped

1 cup thick pizza sauce
4–6 cups dandelion greens,
   washed, drained and chopped
6 oz. sliced mozzarella cheese
2–3 Tbsp. fresh grated Parmesan
   cheese (optional)
1 egg white
2 tsp. water
2 tsp. fennel seeds

Place 2½ cups flour in medium bowl. Add yeast, oil, sugar, salt and hot water and stir until dough starts to form into a ball, adding flour if needed. Place dough on lightly floured work surface and knead in as much of the remaining flour as needed to make a stiff, smooth dough. Cover dough on board and allow to rest 15 minutes. Meanwhile, grease a baking sheet and sprinkle with cornmeal, shaking to dust evenly. Move dough off the work surface and sprinkle the floured surface with rosemary. Return dough to the floured surface. Roll dough into a 16- x 8-inch rectangle. Some of the rosemary will become imbedded in the bottom of the crust. Along the center of the dough, place the pizza sauce in a strip, spreading evenly. Then place the dandelion greens on the sauce and place the cheeses on top of the greens.

Cut the dough on the sides into 1½ inch strips along the length of the dough. It will resemble a fringe. Starting at one end, take one strip and pull it over the top of the cheeses, angling it down slightly. Take the strip from the other side and pull it over the first strip in the same fashion. Each strip will hold the strip that came before. Repeat with remaining strips until finished. Pinch the last strips and tuck under slightly to hold them in place.

Place prepared sheet next to loaf and, working carefully, place hands under loaf and lift the dough and place it on the sheet at an angle. Cover loaf and place over roasting pan half filled with boiling water. Allow dough to rise 15 minutes. Combine egg white with water and brush over loaf. Sprinkle with fennel seeds and bake in a preheated 375° F oven for 20–25 minutes, or until browned. Cool slightly before slicing. Serves 6–8.

Variation: You can add a little crumbled cooked bacon or cooked Italian sausage on the dandelion greens for a more "deluxe" pizza. Whatever pizza toppings you like can be used—olives, peppers, onions and/or mushrooms—but be careful. You have to lift and move this bread when it is raw. If you add too much filling, it will be impossible to move. Keep weight of fillings to under 1½ pounds.

—PETER GAIL, REPRINTED WITH PERMISSION FROM
THE GREAT DANDELION COOKBOOK

Yellow Dock
(Rumex crispus)

Another pot herb high in vitamins and minerals, young yellow dock leaves can be gathered in the spring and fall. Cold weather seems to improve the taste. Try yellow dock leaves as a substitute for dandelion in the recipe on page 119. Yellow dock root is widely respected because of its high iron content and value in treating anemia, digestive ailments, chronic constipation and liver and gall-bladder ailments.

YELLOW DOCK SEED BREAD

2 cups water
½ cup molasses
¼ cup butter
½ cup coarse cornmeal
4½–5 cups flour (½ whole
    wheat, ½ unbleached bread
    flour)

1½ tsp. salt
½ cup yellow dock seed
1 package dry yeast
½ cup warm water

Bring 2 cups water, molasses and butter to a boil in a saucepan. Lightly sprinkle on cornmeal. Cool 2½ minutes, stirring constantly to prevent lumps. Remove from heat and cool for 30 minutes to about 120° F. Combine 2 cups of flour with the salt and yellow dock seed. Add yeast to warm water and proof for 10 minutes, then stir.

Gradually pour cooled cornmeal mixture into flour mixture and beat with electric mixer at low speed to blend. Add yeast and beat 2 minutes at medium speed to make a thicker batter. Stir in rest of flour to make a soft dough. Knead on floured surface about 10 minutes, adding flour, if needed, until dough is smooth and elastic.

Place in greased bowl, turning to coat, cover with waxed paper and a towel and let rise until doubled in bulk. Punch down, break in half, let rest 10–15 minutes. Shape loaves, place loaves in 9- x 5-inch pans; cover again and let rise until double, about 1 hour. Bake in a preheated 400° F oven for 30–40 minutes. Cool before slicing. Makes 2 loaves.

—Feather Jones, Rocky Mountain Center for Botanical Studies

Flax Bread

To enhance the nutritional quality of your freshly baked bread add 2 to 4 tablespoons of freshly ground flaxseed per loaf. This won't affect the texture of the bread, although it's not recommended for crusty French breads or rolls because flaxseed adds moisture and oil. (See page 202 for more about flaxseeds.)

—CATHY GILEADI-SWEET

BUTTERS

BLACK WALNUT HONEY BUTTER

I like to serve this nut butter warm to show off its unique fragrance. The aromatic black walnuts, salt and honey will pull your taste buds in three different directions!

2 cups shelled black walnut meats*
⅜ tsp. salt
3½ Tbsp. honey

Spread the nut meats out on a baking tray and gently roast in a regular or toaster oven at 200° F for ½ hour. Make sure the nut meats don't burn or get overcooked. Place the roasted nut meats in a food processor along with the salt and honey and blend for several minutes until well mixed and peanut butter-like in texture (it will be somewhat grainier). Makes approximately 12 ounces.

—RUSS COHEN

Black Walnut
(*Juglans nigra*)

After all the hard work of cracking the hulls and shells of black walnuts, it's satisfying to know you can use the hulls for medicine. The hulls are popular for their astringent and antifungal properties. Make a decoction (see page 32) of the hulls and use as a wash against ringworm, athlete's foot or jock itch. Black walnut hulls can also be used internally to treat candidiasis.

*Black walnut shells are notoriously hard to crack (the shells are in fact so hard that they are used commercially as an industrial abrasive). Most conventional nut crackers cannot open black walnuts (even the heavy-duty kind). Unless you have a nutcracker that is specifically designed to handle black walnuts, I advise using a hammer.

GARLIC BUTTER

1 stick butter
3 garlic cloves
1 tsp. Italian seasoning
2 bay leaves

Thickly slice butter into small skillet. Press garlic and add along with the rest of the ingredients. Warm gently for at least 20 minutes. Remove bay leaves before serving. Stir periodically to keep herbs well mixed. Or, you can purée when slightly hardened in a food processor. Serve on French bread, baked potatoes, or any way you would use regular butter. Makes ½ cup.

—Harvest McCampbell

RASPBERRY LEMON VERBENA BUTTER

½ lb. unsalted butter
4 oz. fresh or frozen raspberries (not in syrup)
1 Tbsp. sugar, or to taste
1 small handful small, tender lemon verbena leaves

Thaw the raspberries (if frozen), and pour off excess liquid. With all ingredients at room temperature, blend butter, sugar and raspberries until smooth. This may take a while. Add lemon verbena leaves to taste. You may either grind them up a little or leave them whole. Dried leaves can be used, but use fewer of them as the taste is stronger. Makes 1¼ cup.

—JULIE MANCHESTER

Better Butter

1 cup butter
1 cup flaxseed, canola or olive oil

Blend ingredients in a blender until smooth. (Fresh herbs can be added if desired. My favorites are basil and dill.) Place in a container and label. Keep in the refrigerator. This is easier to spread, contains half the saturated fat and tastes just as good as one-hundred-percent butter. Makes 2 cups.

—RISA MORNIS

HERB BUTTER

½ lb. organic butter
1 tsp. fresh lemon juice
Salt
Dried oregano or basil

3 handfuls each fresh lettuce
   leaves, parsley and onion
   greens
1 handful dandelion leaves

Warm butter slightly, then stir in (with a fork) the lemon juice, some salt and some dried oregano or basil. Mince all the greens finely, put into a mortar and pour the butter mixture into it; then pound all very well with the pestle. A food processor can also be used. Spread on whole wheat toast or use as a sandwich filling. Makes 1½ cups.

—Juliette de Bairacli Levy

VEGETABLES

DANDELION ITALIANO

Pick and thoroughly wash a "mess" of dandelion leaves. Avoid picking from roadsides, under power lines or in areas that have been sprayed with weed killers. Hold greens in parallel bunches and chop into half-inch pieces. Put all the chopped leaves into a pan, cover them with boiling water and then set the pan over heat until the water boils again. Drain off the water. Repeat this process once or twice more. If the greens need more cooking, add a small amount of boiling water and steam for a few minutes. Drain them well, then add several tablespoons of vinegar, a good coating of olive oil, some salt or tamari and (optional) lots of minced garlic or garlic powder. Stir well, taste and correct seasoning (you'll probably need to add more vinegar). This makes a tangy, slightly bitter addition to any meal.

—SUSUN WEED, REPRINTED WITH PERMISSION FROM
WISE WOMAN HERBAL FOR THE CHILDBEARING YEARS.

Bitter Tastes

Bitters used to be a regular part of the human diet. Salads were rich in bitter greens, and bitter tonics were taken regularly to stimulate digestion. Where did our bitter tastes go?

The bitter flavor stimulates the flow of internal juices, helping the digestion and detoxification of the body and the functioning of the liver and pancreas. Eating bitter greens can also lessen the craving for sweets. Because of this, I am in full agreement with herbalist James Green, who states in *The Male Herbal,* that the avoidance and lack of a daily bitter flavor in the Western diet is a primary cause of male and female sexual organ problems and immune system deficiencies. The following wild and cultivated bitters are a few of the many herbs that can be added to salads, soups, casseroles and other foods: dandelion greens, chicory greens, beet and carrot greens, watercress, plantain leaves and yellowdock leaves.

ROASTED GARLIC POTATOES

2 pounds small round colored potatoes (try blue, rose gold or Yukon gold)
½ cup peeled garlic cloves
⅓ cup olive oil
8 sprigs fresh rosemary leaves
Salt and pepper to taste

Wash potatoes. Process garlic, oil and rosemary leaves for about 1 minute until well blended. Mix sauce with potatoes. Add desired salt and pepper. Bake at 425° F for 50 minutes or longer, depending on the size and kind of potatoes used. Serves 6–8.

—JILL YECK, PECONIC RIVER HERB FARM

SEA VEGETA-BALLS

A delightful way to ensure that your body is receiving concentrated amounts of important nutrients such as potassium, iron, magnesium, calcium and iodine. Used extensively in Japan and by coastal dwelling herbalists, kelp and other sea vegetables have long served as a superior nutrient for the thyroid and the endocrine system as a whole.

1 oz. dried kelp, dulse or other sea vegetable	1 small onion
2 cups rolled oats	1 clove fresh garlic
1 cup sunflower seeds	½ cup tahini (sesame paste)

Soak sea vegetables in cold water for at least 5 minutes. Place oats, sunflower seeds, onion and garlic in a food processor and blend until smooth. Drain sea vegetable, chop, add to food processor and purée with other vegetables. Last, add the tahini a bit at a time until mixture sticks together. Pull out 2-inch clumps of mixture and roll into balls on the palm of your hand. Place on greased cookie sheet and bake at 450° F for 25 minutes or until golden brown. Turn balls over after the first 10 minutes of baking.

This should yield about 2 dozen balls which can be served fresh out of the oven or stored in the refrigerator for several days. Use like falafel or meatballs in a sandwich or over pasta. Also makes a special side dish if served in broth or gravy. For a full herbal experience, try sea vegeta-balls served over cooked barley and topped with Chili-Basil Sauce. (See page 97.)

—ANDREA MURRAY

STEAMED NETTLES

8 cups fresh nettles*
1 onion, chopped and sautéed in
2 tsp. olive oil
2 cloves garlic, crushed
Liver-happy gomashio (page 142) to taste

Steam the nettles in a pot of water, strain and combine with the sautéed onion and crushed garlic. Add gomashio to taste. Serves 2–4.

—Ruth Dreier

EGGPLANT & MUSTARD

This is a cold-weather tummy pleaser which can be made richer by adding potato chunks and/or chicken for a main dish. It is great over fish, fowl or tofu cubes or as a side dish.

1 large eggplant, cubed or sliced into strips
3 Tbsp. whole wheat flour
¼ cup cornmeal (try blue)
1 Tbsp. poultry seasoning
2 tsp. each curry powder, onion powder and dried thyme

¼ cup olive oil
3–4 Tbsp. prepared mustard to taste
1½ cup water
1 cup regular or sprouted sunflower seeds

Steam the eggplant for 15 minutes. Meanwhile mix all other ingredients together, except the water and sunflower seeds, in a pot or double boiler. Make a paste and thin with the water to prevent lumps. Bring to a boil to thicken and add the steamed eggplant and sunflower seeds. Serves 6–8.

—Maia Ballis, reprinted with permission
from the Sun Mountain Natural Foods Cookbook.

*See page 50 for more information about nettles and how to harvest them.

CARROTS WITH CUMIN AND GINGER

1 lb. carrots	1 Tbsp. cumin seeds
2 oz. butter	½ oz. fresh chopped ginger
½ oz. brown sugar	Salt and pepper
½ Tbsp. white wine vinegar	2 Tbsp. fresh chopped parsley

Cook carrots. Melt butter with sugar and vinegar. Add cumin seeds, ginger and salt and pepper to taste. Toss with freshly cooked carrots and sprinkle with parsley. Serves 4.

—JANE CARDEN

FAVORITE FAST CABBAGE

Ready to eat in 15 minutes. For variety substitute thinly sliced kale, collards or Brussels sprouts for the cabbage or add fresh ginger, fresh burdock root or fresh wild mushrooms.

4 oz. seaweed (hijiki, sea palm fronds or alaria)
2 cups hot water
1 onion, sliced from top to bottom like crescent moons
1 Tbsp. olive oil

2 cups finely sliced or shredded cabbage
1 carrot grated
1 Tbsp. tamari (soy sauce)
4 Tbsp. sunflower seeds

Soak seaweed in 2 cups hot water. On low heat, sauté onion in oil. While it cooks, shred cabbage. When onion is limp and translucent, add cabbage and cook another 5 minutes. Stir several times while you grate carrot and drain seaweed. (Reserve soaking water.) Arrange grated carrot in a circle on top of the cabbage and onion. Put seaweed in the center of the carrot circle. Add tamari and 3–4 tablespoons of seaweed soaking water to the skillet. Cover tightly. Raise heat and cook until steam appears, then lower heat and cook another 5 minutes or until carrots are tender. Meanwhile, toast the sunflower seeds. Spread seeds liberally over dish before serving. Serves 4–6.

—Susun Weed. Reprinted with permission
from *Breast Cancer? Breast Health!*

GERMAN CABBAGE

½ cup virgin olive oil (enough
    to coat all the cabbage)
1 cabbage cored and chopped
1 tsp. salt
Pepper to taste

Fresh dandelion, alfalfa, mallow
    and nettles
¼ cup cider vinegar
¼ cup water

Place oil in a large warm skillet and add cabbage, salt and pepper. Cut
herbs into small pieces and add. Simmer on medium heat, turning and
blending cabbage for 10–15 minutes. Add vinegar and water. Simmer at
low heat until tender. Enjoy!

—FEATHER JONES, ROCKY MOUNTAIN CENTER FOR BOTANICAL STUDIES

GINGER DANDELION BUDS

2 cups of fresh dandelion blos-
    soms
1 egg beaten
1 cup milk
1 cup flour

Pepper to taste
2 tsp. grated ginger
3 fresh lemon balm leaves,
    chopped
Olive oil for pan

Gather dandelion blossoms just before you make this. If that is not possible, they will store for a day or two in a plastic bag in the refrigerator.
Fresh is best! In a bowl, combine all the ingredients except the dandelion
blossoms and olive oil. Heat a little bit of olive oil over low heat in a frying
pan. Be careful; once this heats up it can splatter. Remove the dandelion
stems right up to the base of the blossom. Dip the blossoms in the batter
and, flower head first, push them down into the bottom of the pan. This
way, even if the blossoms have wilted shut, they will look nice and big and
appear to be open. Cook, until golden brown, flipping them to cook on
both sides. Serve. They are delicious eaten plain or accompanied with an
herbal mustard. Great as a snack, at a brunch or a buffet. Include them in
all your spring celebrations. Serves 4.

—RACHEL SCHNEIDER, FLOWER POWER HERBALS

MASHED POTATOES WITH NETTLES

Harvest the nettles when they are at most 1 foot high, using leather gloves and a pair of scissors. To get a steady supply of nettles during summer you can cut them down about once a month so you'll always have new tender growth. Depending on the amount of nettles you have collected, you may need to prepare them in batches.

Cover the nettles with water and wait for about 10 minutes to allow any spiders and caterpillars to leave. Then put the drained green shoots into boiling salted water. Boil until the stem turns bright green; this doesn't take long. Take out of the water and add the next batch of presoaked and drained nettles. What you can't eat today you should either freeze or dry. Cut nettles into very small pieces and add to mashed potatoes.

—HENRIETTA KRESS

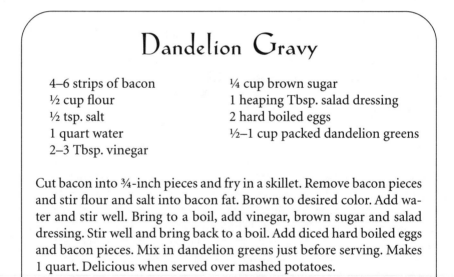

Dandelion Gravy

4–6 strips of bacon
½ cup flour
½ tsp. salt
1 quart water
2–3 Tbsp. vinegar

¼ cup brown sugar
1 heaping Tbsp. salad dressing
2 hard boiled eggs
½–1 cup packed dandelion greens

Cut bacon into ¾-inch pieces and fry in a skillet. Remove bacon pieces and stir flour and salt into bacon fat. Brown to desired color. Add water and stir well. Bring to a boil, add vinegar, brown sugar and salad dressing. Stir well and bring back to a boil. Add diced hard boiled eggs and bacon pieces. Mix in dandelion greens just before serving. Makes 1 quart. Delicious when served over mashed potatoes.

—PETER GAIL, REPRINTED FROM *THE GREAT DANDELION COOKBOOK*

ZUCCHINI ROUNDS

These can be prepared several hours in advance. Keep refrigerated and bake before serving.

5 small zucchini	Basil leaves
¼ lb. mozzarella cheese, cut in small pieces	Parmesan cheese
1 pint cherry tomatoes, sliced thinly	Black pepper

Wash zucchini and slice ½-inch thick. Scoop out center of slices, leaving the bottom intact. Place ½ teaspoon of mozzarella cheese on each and top with a cherry tomato slice, basil leaf and a sprinkle of Parmesan cheese and pepper. Place in oven at 400° F for 5–7 minutes, just until cheese is melted but not brown. Serve immediately. Serves 4–6.

—JUDITH GRAVES, LAMBS & THYME

GRILLED VEGETABLE MEDLEY

Oil or softened butter
4 medium yellow squash, sliced
3 medium tomatoes, cut into
small wedges
1 small onion, thinly sliced
½ small zucchini, cut into cubes
2 cups broccoli florettes

2 large carrots, cut into thin
strips
*Epicurean Delights No-salt
Herb & Spice Blend
1–3 Tbsp. oil/lemon juice combination

Coat a large piece of heavy-duty aluminum foil with oil or butter. Place vegetables on foil, trying to get a double layer. Salt lightly and sprinkle with herb and spice blend. Pour lemon juice and oil over vegetables and wrap tightly in foil. Put over medium coals on grill. Turn and check after 15 minutes for desired tenderness. Serves 4.

—ALLIE LETSON, THE POTTED HERB

*Epicurean Delights No-salt Herb & Spice Blend is available via mail order from *The Potted Herb* and contains onion and garlic powder, tarragon, celery leaf flakes, oregano, parsley, paprika, kelp, savory, thyme, rosemary, basil, marjoram, bay leaves, sage, lemon peel powder and black pepper.

ONIONS & THYME

1 lb. small white onions
8 cloves
2 tsp. brown sugar
1 tsp. salt
2 tsp. butter

½ cup flour
1 cup milk
1 tsp. dried thyme or 1 Tbsp.
  finely cut fresh thyme

Place just enough cold water in pan with onions to prevent burning. Then add cloves, brown sugar and salt. Cover pan and cook slowly until onions are soft.

To make the white thyme sauce, heat the butter slowly in a double boiler until melted. Beat the flour into the butter until it is all blended. Then slowly add the warmed milk, keeping it on a low heat until the mixture thickens. Blend in the thyme. (You can also make the sauce with parsley or garlic.) Pour the sauce over the drained onions. Serves 6–8.

—JULIETTE DE BAIRACLI LEVY, REPRINTED WITH PERMISSION
FROM *NATURE'S CHILDREN*

MAIN DISHES

Eating food is a very personal physical and emotional activity that we all go through every day of our lives. What we eat is often our own choice, a control that does not always extend to other areas of our lives. When someone tries to tell us what to eat or tell us not to eat what we love, our defenses rise and we may consume our favorite food in anger and rebellion. This kind of negativity always backfires. Rather than preach the benefits of food nutrition, the recipes in this book attempt to offer new delicious tastes that can be added to your comfortable old ways of eating, providing interesting and healthful new culinary experiences.

Sometimes we get so wrapped up in our own eating habits we stop experimenting and trying new tastes. How will you know you like or dislike a food if you've never tried it?

Everything worthwhile takes a little extra effort. The herbalists in this book offer these recipes as inspiration. Some are easy, some are complicated, but almost all of them take you outside for fresh air and herbs!

CURRIED WILD GREENS

The secret to this recipe is to have a freshly ground spicy curry mixture (see page 133). I like this recipe because it's quick and easy. I can serve it simply or dress it up with condiments typically used in East India, such as coconut, raisins, yogurt and chutney.

3–4 quarts wild greens (favorites for this dish are chickweed, amaranth, lamb's quarters, nettle, purslane, watercress and mustard)
2 Tbsp. butter
2 Tbsp. flour
2 cloves garlic, minced
1 Tbsp. curry mixture
1 cup milk
1 Tbs. Butter
1 onion
Cashews, raisins, coconut to taste
4 cups cooked rice

Wash fresh greens well and chop into small pieces. Steam and allow to drain. Melt butter in a skillet and brown the flour, stirring all the while. When nicely browned, add garlic and curry mixture. Mix in well, then remove from heat. Very slowly, stir in milk, mixing well. If you pour it in too quickly you will have those notorious lumps. Return to heat and add steamed greens. Cook over low heat until sauce thickens to desired consistency. In a separate skillet, sauté an onion in butter until golden brown. Add curry, cashews, raisins and coconut to taste. Cook a few minutes to merge flavors. You may have to add more butter. Stir in cooked rice. Serve sauce over rice. The sauce can also be served over toast. Serves 4–6.

—ROSEMARY GLADSTAR SLICK, REPRINTED WITH PERMISSION
FROM *SAGE MOUNTAIN WILD FOODS*

Lamb's Quarters

Lamb's quarters (*Chenopodium album*) or pigweed is a common garden weed that contains more vitamins and minerals than spinach plus more protein and calcium than any other green vegetable; yet most gardeners throw this plant into the compost heap! Also called goosefoot or wild spinach, the leaves are shaped somewhat like the print of a goose's webbed foot. They are blue-green on top with a white powdery coating on the bottom. A tasty mild-flavored green, lamb's quarters can be eaten raw or cooked. The seeds of the plant are also edible and yield a good cereal food. They can be harvested in late summer and early fall, when they begin to dry. Hold a cloth under the plant and rub the heads to free the seeds. Winnow away the husks by pouring the seed back and forth between two containers in front of a fan or in a good breeze. Roast the seeds in a 300° F oven for an hour, cool and grind in a clean coffee mill until they are of a fine or medium consistency. Cook as a breakfast cereal, or mix with regular flour for baking.

Curry

These mixes begin with ground spices which may be purchased in bulk, but they may have been sitting on the shelf in the store for some time before you buy them. For freshness, it is better to use ground spice from a can or you can purchase whole spices and grind them yourself, using a spice grinder or a coffee grinder (not one that you're using for coffee). Store mix in a tight-lidded jar in a dark place.

Mild Curry Blend

A mild blend and a good starting point for experimenting.

4 Tbsp. ground coriander
3 Tbsp. ground turmeric
2 Tbsp. ground cumin
½ Tbsp. garlic powder

Pungent Curry Blend

This starts with the basic four but adds ginger, mustard and black pepper for pungency; red chili powder for sharpness and cardamom for an additional aromatic sweetness.

4 Tbsp. coriander
2 Tbsp. turmeric
1½ Tbsp. cumin
1 Tbsp. fenugreek
1½ tsp. each black pepper, poppy seeds, ginger, red chili
¾ tsp. dried mustard
½ tsp. cardamom

—SUSAN WITTIG ALBERT, REPRINTED WITH PERMISSION
FROM *MARVELOUS MUSTARDS & CURIOUS CURRIES.*

CURRIED CHICKEN-OF-THE-WOODS

¼ cup butter or olive oil
2 lbs. chicken-of-the-woods
　　mushrooms (*Polyporus sul-*
　　phureus), sliced
Sea salt
1 medium onion, chopped
1 medium green pepper,
　　chopped
2 cloves garlic, chopped

1 Tbsp. curry powder
16 oz. canned tomatoes, with
　　liquid
½ cup currants
¼ cup toasted almonds
4 cups cooked brown rice
Chutney (See page 95 for a
　　chutney recipe)

Melt butter in a large skillet over low heat. Brown mushrooms, turning pieces occasionally. Season with salt to taste. Remove mushrooms when browned and set aside. Sauté onion and green pepper, adding garlic and curry powder. Return mushrooms to skillet and add tomatoes. Cover and cook until hot and bubbly. Stir in currants and almonds. Serve over hot rice with chutney. Serves 4–6.

—Gail Ulrich, Blazing Star Herbal School

CURRIED WILD RICE WITH LENTILS

1 medium onion, chopped
2 cloves garlic, chopped
2 Tbsp. oil
5–6 dried shiitake mushrooms
1 cup wild rice blend
½ cup red lentils

½ cup green lentils
4 cups water
¼ tsp. each salt, ground corian-
　　der and cinnamon
½ tsp. each curry and cumin
Dash of red pepper

Sauté onions and garlic in oil. Break up mushrooms and add to the sauté. When soft, add rice and lentils, stir and brown for 1 minute. Add the water and seasonings. Bring to a boil, cover and simmer for 45–50 minutes. Stir once. You may need to add more water. Serve warm with a fresh salad and whole grain bread for a hearty meal. Serves 4.

—Jane Smolnik

Shiitake Mushrooms

The shiitake mushroom is one of the most highly prized foods in Oriental cuisine. Its rich, caramel-like flavor lends itself well to seasonings, sauces and soups. Shiitake has also been used in folk treatments for colds and measles and is currently used to help lower blood cholesterol levels and prevent heart disease. Shiitake is valuable in bolstering the immune system to increase the body's ability to ward off cancerous tumors, AIDS and viral infections.

HERBED RICE

My family started eating lots of rice when my husband discovered he had allergies to several other grains. Rice is nice but it can get pretty boring. Out of desperation, I began adding a different culinary herb to the rice every night— usually thyme, basil, lemon balm, parsley or oregano. The immediate benefit was that we enjoyed a variety of tasty dishes. However, it wasn't until a few months later that we noticed a hidden benefit. All around us, folks were suffering with the normal colds, flus and sinus infections. We remained well for the entire winter for the first time in our lives. This is herbal medicine at its best— staying healthy though the foods we eat.

Place cooked rice in a skillet with 2 tablespoons of olive or canola oil and sauté until some of the rice begins to get crispy. Add the herbs of your choice (2–3 Tbsp. fresh herbs for 3–4 cups of rice), stir well, turn off heat and cover for a few minutes.

—TINA FINNEYFROCK

NETTLES-TEMPEH MELT

I first made this rejuvenating supper to bring my strength back after a miscarriage. It's wonderfully nourishing, absolutely delicious and quick to prepare.

1 8 oz. cake 3-grain tempeh	6 garlic cloves, crushed
¼–½ cup olive oil	4 wild leeks, chopped
Tamari or soy sauce	16 oz. fresh nettle leaves,
6 oz. fresh shiitake mushrooms,	chopped
sliced	1 cup grated soy cheddar cheese

Slice the tempeh horizontally into 2 thin sheets. Cut these into quarters to make 8 tempeh strips. Heat olive oil in a large skillet with a cover. Place tempeh into hot oil and brown on high heat. Turn tempeh. Sprinkle with tamari to taste. Add shiitake mushrooms and cook until browned. Add garlic and wild leeks. Top with nettles and sprinkle cheese over all. Place cover on pot and reduce heat to a simmer. Cook until nettles wilt and cheese melts, about 3–5 minutes. Serve hot. Serves 2–3.

—Gail Ulrich, Blazing Star Herbal School

DANDELION PIZZA SANDWICH

On a piece of mini pita bread or toasted English muffin, put a coating of spaghetti or pizza sauce, a heaping pile of chopped raw dandelion leaves and a covering of cheese. Place in the microwave or broiler until the cheese melts.

—PETER GAIL, REPRINTED WITH PERMISSION
FROM *THE GREAT DANDELION COOKBOOK*

MUSHROOM BURGER

Rice mozzarella cheese or tofu
   American cheese
Whole wheat seeded bun
Mushrooms, any kind, sliced
Water
Soy sauce
Sprouts, tomatoes or other gar-
   nish

Guacamole
1 ripe avocado
1 scallion, chopped
1 clove garlic, minced
Parmesan cheese, to taste

Put a slice of cheese on top of the bun and run it under the broiler until melted. Simmer the sliced mushrooms in a little water with soy sauce for about 5 minutes. To make guacamole, mash an avocado with the chopped scallion, some chopped garlic and Parmesan cheese. Spread a thick layer of the guacamole on the bottom bun. Use a slotted spoon to scoop out the mushrooms, and pile them on the guacamole. Add the sprouts, any other additions you like (tomatoes, etc.) and cover with the top bun. Have plenty of napkins ready . . . this is a challenge to eat neatly!

—SHARON MURPHY

DANDY BURGERS

1 cup packed dandelion flowers
(milky bottom section re-
moved)
½ cup flour
¼–⅜ cup milk (enough to make
stiff batter)

¼ cup chopped onion
½ tsp. each salt and garlic powder
¼ tsp. each basil and oregano
⅛ tsp. pepper
Oil for frying

To prepare dandelions, trim and save yellow petals, discarding green bot-
toms. Mix all ingredients with enough milk to form a stiff batter. Roll into
golf ball-size pieces and flatten to ½-inch thick. Pan fry, turning until crisp
on both sides. Serves 2–4.

—Peter Gail, reprinted from *The Great Dandelion Cookbook*

FLOWER FRITTERS

1½ cups dandelion flowers
2 eggs, beaten
1 cup sour cream
1½ cups corn meal
1 tsp. baking powder

1 Tbsp. fresh rosemary flowers
¼ cup wild onions, chopped
1 cup grated cheese
¼ cup water

Remove green caps and stems from dandelion flowers. Combine beaten
eggs and sour cream and add to flowers. Add remaining ingredients. Drop
by spoonfuls onto hot oiled frying pan. Brown on both sides. Serve hot.
Makes 10–12 3-inch fritters.

—Vickie Shufer

CARDOONS

These are the young tender stems of first-year burdock plants and make the base for a complete meal.

Eggs or flaxseed oil, whisked until frothy

Parmesan or other grated hard cheese

Wheat germ or soy flour

Burdock stems. Peel strings if tough and slice into pot. (These stems will brown if left in the open air, so let sit in water until ready to cook.)

Mix the first two ingredients, about 1 Tbsp. of cheese to 1 egg. Add wheat germ or flour. Add seasoning as desired. Try Italian seasoning, salt and pepper. Parboil burdock stems in a small amount of water in a covered pan for about 5 minutes. Drain stems, then flour lightly. Dip in batter and stirfry in oil quickly. Eat as it is or serve with a sauce. You can also layer in a casserole in place of lasagna noodles with sauce and cheese. Add a layer of steamed wild greens, such as nettle or lamb's quarters, for a truly wild feast.

—Pat Chichon

CHICKPEAS AND ROSES

Make a dried rose blossom infusion with 1 ounce of blossoms (and a handful of rose hips, if you like) steeped covered in 1 quart of boiled water for 1–1½ hours. Cook 1 cup of presoaked chickpeas in the rose infusion until they are soft. Add spices such as cumin, coriander and cardamom, to taste. This is delicious as is, and/or mixed with mild or bitter cooked greens and sassafras rice.

—Robin Rose Bennett, *Wise Woman Healing Ways*

BURDOCK WITH MISO AND LEMON PEEL

2 Tbsp. sesame oil
2½ cups thin rounds fresh
  burdock root
1–2 Tbsp. miso paste

3–6 Tbsp. water
3 Tbsp. white sesame seeds,
  toasted
1 tsp. minced lemon peel

Heat a heavy skillet and coat with oil. Sauté burdock rounds until their strong aroma is no longer released. Add water to cover, bring to a boil and cover pan. Cook until tender, adding water occasionally if necessary. Thin miso in 3–6 Tbs. water and add to pan when burdock is ready. Simmer, stirring over very low heat, until all liquid has evaporated. Add sesame seeds and lemon peel; sauté 1–2 minutes more. For balance serve with steamed greens, such as spinach, collards, kale or nettles.

—DONNA D'TERRA

Simple Flax Topping

If you make a stir-fry or any other rice dish, grind some flaxseed and sprinkle it on top. The taste is mild and nutty and it's a pleasant way to get your essential fatty acids.

—CATHI GILEADI-SWEET

RUTH'S BURDOCK AND BROWN RICE DINNER

A marvelously satisfying dinner that leaves you full to the brim!

1–2 oz. hijiki seaweed
2 Tbsp. tamari soy sauce
1 cup thinly sliced fresh burdock
    root
1 cup thinly sliced carrots
3 Tbsp. sesame seeds

2 pinches thyme
¼ cup chopped fresh chickweed
    and/or violet leaves, lamb's
    quarters, dandelion or parsley
2 cups cooked brown rice

Pour boiling water over hijiki to cover by ¼ inch; add the tamari and let marinate for 24 hours. In a separate pot, steam thinly sliced burdock root for 5 minutes; then add the carrots. Cook until tender. My favorite wild green for this dish is chickweed. Its moist texture complements the rice and seaweed nicely. Mix hijiki, burdock, carrots, sesame seeds and greens together. Serve on top of freshly cooked rice. Sprinkle with thyme. Serves 4–6

—RUTH DREIER

Liver-happy Gomashio

Use equal parts of:

Milk thistle seeds
Tamari to taste
Sesame seeds
Powdered kelp

Sauté whole milk thistle seeds in a frying pan over low heat until the seeds are cooked. You will feel how much lighter they become as you stir them in the pan. Add tamari soy sauce and let it cook into the seeds until they soak it all up. Let cool and grind seeds to a powder (use a small electric coffee grinder or blender). Also grind equal parts of sesame seeds and dried kelp. Mix ingredients together and keep on the table for flavoring soups, salads, vegetables, etc. See page 54 for another version of Gomashio

—RUTH DREIER

BURDOCK KIMPIRA

1½ Tbsp. sesame oil
1 cup each burdock root and carrots, cut into thin matchsticks
Dash sea salt
2 Tbsp. shoyu or tamari

Heat a heavy skillet and coat with sesame oil. Add the burdock sticks, which should sizzle softly as soon as they touch the surface of the pan. Sauté over medium heat until they no longer release their strong aroma. Stir constantly. Add carrots, sauté for 1 or 2 minutes longer, then add enough water to cover the bottom of the pan. Cover pan and reduce heat; simmer 25–30 minutes, or until vegetables are tender, adding water occasionally if necessary. Season to taste with salt. Serves 4.

—DONNA D'TERRA

Burdock
(*Articum lappa*)

Another common weed much loved by herbalists, burdock is highly valued as both medicine and food. Called *gobo* in Japan, the fresh root has a sweet taste and sticky texture. Used fresh, as a nourishing tonic, burdock is high in essential minerals and vitamin C. First-year burdock roots are the best tasting and can be harvested up until late spring of their second year (before the flower stalk grows.) Parboiling is suggested for older roots and roots that are not fresh from the ground. Burdock can also be dried and added to beans, rice, soups, stew and other long-cooking dishes.

An important herb for the liver, burdock is used by modern herbalists in formulas for skin diseases and kidney stones, and is a main ingredient in a renowned cancer formula called Essiac.

HERB AND VEGETABLE STIR-FRY

1 head cauliflower, cut into florettes
5 carrots, peeled and sliced thinly
1 bunch broccoli, cut into florettes
1 tsp. ginger powder
¼ tsp. garlic granules
1 tsp. dillweed, snipped fine
6 fresh lemon balm leaves, cut small
1 Tbsp. oil
1 Tbsp. vinegar
2 Tbsp. Worcestershire sauce
1 can condensed tomato soup diluted with ½ can water
1 cup cooked rice

Mix vegetables and herbs and sauté at medium heat in oil. Continue to stir slowly until tender crisp. Add vinegar, Worcestershire sauce and diluted tomato soup. Mix and simmer slowly for a few more minutes and spoon over cooked rice. Serves 16.

—JUDITH GRAVES, *LAMBS & THYME*

Lemon Balm
(*Melissa officinalis*)

This herb will delight your senses and lift your spirits. The lemony leaves replace lemon in drinks and teas and offer a delicious tang to salads. An herb for the nervous system, lemon balm eases anxiety and depression, and relieves a stress-related stomach ache.

PORTABELLO ROMANOFF

A balanced, wholesome meal, drawing from all food groups. Parsley helps digestion and basil is soothing. Don't forget to light the candles, turn on quiet music and serve on special dinnerware!

2 garlic cloves, chopped
4 slices fresh ginger, chopped, but not too small
¼ cup chopped celery
3 Tbsp. olive oil
¼ cup each fresh basil and fresh parsley, or 1 Tbsp. dried
Dash or two curry and/or coriander (optional)
2 portabello mushrooms, sliced
2 medium zucchini, sliced
1 large onion, sliced

1 large carrot, thinly sliced diagonally
3 Tbsp. soy or teriyaki sauce
Salt to taste
4 cups cooked, drained whole wheat noodles or macaroni (still hot)
1 cup low-fat sour cream
Paprika
Parsley or slivered scallions for garnish

In a large pot sauté garlic, ginger and celery in olive oil until partially cooked. Add the basil and parsley and stir together quickly so it doesn't scorch. Sprinkle in the curry and/or coriander. Add the vegetables and stir to coat. Add a little water, a teaspoon at a time, to keep vegetables from sticking; stir and toss while cooking. Add the soy or teriyaki sauce and continue cooking until vegetables are cooked but still crisp. Salt to taste. Turn off heat.

Immediately, add the warm cooked noodles and toss until everything is coated and mixed together. Now add the sour cream and mix well. Sprinkle with a bit of paprika for color, add a garnish of parsley sprigs or a few slivers of scallion. Serve with spinach and feta salad (see page 15). Serves 4.

—KIYRA PAGE

SPICY PEANUT NOODLE SALAD

Seasoned with immune-enhancing garlic, onions, hot peppers and beneficial essential fatty acids (from flaxseed oil), this tasty noodle dish is always a favorite at potluck dinners. You can control the spiciness by adjusting the amount of garlic, hot peppers and chili oil.

12 oz. package of udon noodles (available in Asian food section of grocery stores). Prepare as per package directions
Sauce:
¼ cup soy sauce
¼ cup rice vinegar
3–4 Tbsp. toasted sesame oil
1 Tbsp. flaxseed oil (Use garlic/chili flavored flaxseed oil, if more spice is desired.)

⅛–½ tsp. chili oil
2–4 tsp. freshly minced garlic
⅓ cup chopped green onions
¼–½ tsp. finely chopped chili peppers (Adjust to your taste and be careful to thoroughly wash hands after handling peppers.)
1 cup chopped roasted peanuts

Mix sauce ingredients together and pour over the prepared, drained noodles. Stir the chopped roasted peanuts into the noodle and sauce mixture. It can be served immediately or kept in the refrigerator until ready to serve. Heat or let come to room temperature. I like to let the noodles absorb the sauce for a few hours before serving. Serves 4.

Optional garnishes: Chopped green onions or chives, extra peanuts, a sprinkle of hot peppercorns, spicy, bright nasturtium flowers and/or chive blossoms.

For a lighter version: Double the amount of noodles and do not thoroughly drain them.

—SHARLEEN ANDREWS-MILLER

NANA THERESA'S SPAGHETTI SAUCE

This precious recipe was taught to me by my grandmother who is from Ascoli Piceno, the Marche region of Italy. She learned how to make sauce from her mother, who learned it from her mother, and so on. The recipes have been altered to taste over the years, each person changing them just a little bit. That's why my Great Aunt Mary's sauce tastes different from my Great Aunt Olga's which tastes different from my grandmother's. My husband insists my variation is the best.

15–20 medium ripe tomatoes
  (preferably Roma tomatoes)
1 14-oz. can peeled whole tomatoes
8 cloves
1 medium onion
3 whole cloves of garlic

1 stalk celery
2 bay leaves
2 sprigs fresh sweet basil
1 sprig fresh rosemary
1 sprig fresh oregano
  (or substitute dried herbs)

Blanch and peel fresh tomatoes. Remove seeds. Chop both the fresh and the canned tomatoes briefly in a blender. Pierce the cloves into the onion. In a large pot, combine the tomatoes, onion, garlic, celery and bay leaves and other herbs. Bring to a boil, then turn down to a simmer. Simmer for 1½ hours. Serve over spaghetti. You can also add cooked spare ribs, sausage, pork or meatballs to the sauce. Adding some kind of meat to the sauce while it is cooking adds to the flavor. A meatball recipe follows. Enough for 6–8 servings.

—MELISSA HERTZLER, HONEY BEE GARDENS

MEATBALLS

1–1½ lbs. lean hamburger
2 slices bread, torn into tiny
  pieces
3 garlic cloves, minced
3 eggs
¼ cup Parmesan cheese

1 Tbsp. fresh Italian parsley,
  finely chopped
Freshly ground pepper to taste
Olive oil
1 can tomato paste
Water

In a large bowl, mix together all ingredients except the olive oil, tomato paste and water. Form into meatballs. Heat oil in skillet. Brown meatballs well on all sides. When meatballs are brown, add them to the sauce above, letting them simmer in the sauce for half an hour. After the meatballs are removed from the skillet, add the tomato paste to the skillet along with a can of water. Stir and simmer on low heat until blended. Add to the sauce (on previous page). Makes 18 1½-inch meatballs.

—Melissa Hertzler

NETTLE LASAGNA

1 medium onion, chopped
3–5 garlic cloves, chopped
¼ cup olive oil
3 handfuls dried nettles, crushed
½ Tbsp. kelp, crushed
8–10 fresh or dried shiitake
  mushrooms, chopped
¼ cup pickled dandelion roots,
  chopped*
¼ cup Parmesan cheese

Fresh or dried rosemary, sage,
  oregano and thyme to taste
Crushed tomatoes and tomato
  sauce to make 4 cups
8 cups fresh young nettle tops
9–12 lasagna noodles, boiled
  and drained
¾–1 lb. goat or sheep feta
  cheese, crumbled

Sauté onion and garlic in olive oil until golden. Add everything up to and
including tomato sauce and simmer 1 hour. As sauce is simmering, steam
the fresh nettles for 10–15 minutes, drain and drink the pot liquor (the
cook's reward!). Layer a pan with sauce, cooked lasagna noodles, sauce,
nettles, feta, sauce, noodles, etc., ending with feta as the final topping. Bake
in 350° F for 30 minutes or until bubbly all the way through. Serves 12.

—Suzanne Nagler

*See recipe for pickled dandelion roots, page 13.

EGGPLANT LASAGNA

My recipes have been put together to help regain body chemistry balance according to the pH balance theory. I have used them all for many years. They are both unique and delicious as well as very healthful.

1 clove garlic, chopped	1 medium eggplant
½ cup chopped onion	3 cups ricotta or cottage cheese
1 Tbsp. olive oil	2 eggs, beaten
1 1-lb. can tomatoes	½ cup Parmesan cheese
2 6-oz. cans tomato paste	1 lb. mozzarella, cheese, shred-
3 Tbsp. fresh parsley	ded
1 Tbsp. fresh basil	

Sauté garlic and onion in oil. Add the tomatoes and tomato paste, 1 Tbsp. of the parsley and basil. Simmer for 30 minutes. Peel and slice eggplant into ½-inch slices. Mix together cottage or ricotta cheese, eggs, rest of parsley and Parmesan cheese. Layer in greased backing dish: Eggplant, cottage cheese, mozzarella, sauce, eggplant, cottage cheese, etc. Bake at 375° F for 30 minutes or so. Serves 6.

—Michael Jonas Kahn

SOUTHWEST ANGEL HAIR
& WILD FENNEL

2 handfuls wild, young spring
    fennel leaves or 2 Tbsp. of
    fennel seeds*
Salt
½ tsp. crushed red pepper flakes
1 medium onion, chopped fine
5 Tbsp. extra-virgin olive oil

6 black olives, drained and diced
¼ cup yellow raisins, plumped
    in warm water
Freshly ground black pepper
1 lb. angel hair pasta
½ cup pine nuts, lightly toasted
    and coarsely chopped

Make sure the wild fennel you pick has not been sprayed with pesticides. Wash well and chop into 3-inch pieces. Cook the fennel in boiling salted water for 10 minutes. Set aside 1 cup of the cooking water and reserve the rest in a large pan for cooking the angel hair pasta; then drain the fennel well. Sauté the onion and red pepper flakes in the olive oil for approximately 12 minutes. Stir in the reserved 1 cup cooking water, olives, raisins and the fennel and keep warm over low heat. Bring the large pot of water to a boil, adding more water if necessary, and cook the angel hair pasta according to package directions. When the pasta is done, drain and toss with fennel sauce, top with fresh ground pepper and pine nuts. Serves 5–6.

—JUDY DUNNING & BONNIE PASTOR, SOUTHWEST HERBS

*If wild fennel doesn't grow in your area you can use fennel seeds. Lightly grind 2 Tbsp. seeds in a coffee grinder and then add the ground seeds to the onion and red pepper flakes mixture. Continue as above, substituting a chicken or vegetable stock for the 1 cup of cooking water you need for the sauce.

PESTO PASTA

½ lb. spaghetti, cooked and drained
½ cup pesto (See page 46)
½–1 cup milk, tomato sauce or tomato juice
2 tomatoes, sliced
Grated Parmesan cheese

Warm the pesto and desired liquid together in a skillet. Add more liquid to taste, if needed. Pour green sauce over noodles, place sliced tomatoes on top and sprinkle with Parmesan cheese. Serves 3–4.

—RISA MORNIS

CLOVER NOODLES

1 cup clover flour
Water
5 eggs
1 Tbsp. oil

½ tsp. salt
3–5 cups unbleached white flour
   (or ½ semolina and ½ white)

Put clover flour into a bowl and add enough water to reconstitute to a moist consistency. Add eggs, oil, salt and beat. You should have a slimy green soup. Add white flour to make a stiff dough. Remove to floured surface and knead until it won't tear when you stretch it. Let rest 30 minutes in refrigerator.

Making the Noodles

Hand-cranked pasta machine: Cut dough into about seven or eight equal-sized balls and run through pasta machine. Start on setting #1 and then press through 2, 3 and 5. Add flour with each run through the machine to avoid sticking.

Electric pasta machine: Clover noodles can be made by using the recipe that comes with the machine except replace 2 Tbsp. of white flour with 2 Tbsp. of clover flour. Adjust the liquid as necessary to get the right texture (pebbly pea-shaped pieces), extrude and serve.

Handmade noodles: Roll out on floured pastry sheets to about ⅛-inch thick. Decide the length you want and make horizontal cuts in the dough, roll each row from bottom toward the top and slice each spiral of dough into the width you want—⅛-inch, ¼-inch width or your choice.

Store extra noodles in your freezer or dry on the racks of a food dryer or over a coat hanger.

For added color, make one batch with beet juice and one without green flour. Use all three colors for a delightful pasta salad.

—ALTHEA DIXON

Making Green Flours

To make green flours, harvest fresh green leaves of your favorite green (spinach, amaranth, clover, etc.). Rinse in cold fresh water and let drain. Place leaves on a stainless steel or parchment-lined cookie sheet. Dry in oven on the lowest heat until dry and crisp to the touch. Put in the blender at high speed, then sift out larger stems and pieces.

Remaining flour is used in ratio of 1 to 4 for making noodles—1 part green flour to 4 parts white flour. In bread recipes, start with a 1 to 32 ratio. If the recipe calls for 8 cups of flour use ¼ cup green flour. As you become accustomed to using green flours you can make your own adjustments to suit your taste. Store green flours up to a year in glass jars in a cool, dark place.

NETTLE LOAF

3 cups steamed nettles, puréed
2 Tbsp. each chopped celery and onion
2 Tbsp. butter
2½ cups cooked brown rice
3 eggs, beaten

Combine all ingredients, pour into a well-greased loaf pan and bake at 350° F for 30 minutes. Serve with a white sauce or pesto sauce. Serves 4–5.

—MARY BOVE

LENTIL LOAF

2 cups lentils, cooked and
   drained
½ tsp. vegetable salt
½ cup wheat germ
½ tsp. cumin (optional)
½ cup whole wheat bread
   crumbs

2 eggs, lightly beaten
1 cup evaporated milk or yogurt
½ cup chopped onions
3 Tbsp. oil

Slightly mash cooked lentils in a large bowl. Add remaining ingredients and mix well. Place in a greased 9-inch baking dish. Bake at 350° for 45 minutes. Cut into 9 squares.

—MICHAEL JONAS KAHN

FAIRY FOOD CASSEROLE

A dish made almost entirely of wild foods that can be found almost anywhere in the garden or wayside. Guaranteed to bring the magic of nature into your life.

2 cups raw wild rice
Handful wild oregano
2 Tbsp. wild mint
1 Tbsp. wild catnip
1 cup wild purslane
6 wild onions
5 leaves garden basil
3 cloves garlic (2 cloves for rice,
    1 clove for mushrooms)

1 cup wild mushrooms, chopped
2 tsp. olive oil
Goat's cheese
1 Tbsp. wild mustard seeds
3 Tbsp. yellow dock seeds
Handful of wild flowers

Boil rice until done and set aside. Collect your wild herbs and mushrooms. Chop herbs, purslane, wild onions, basil and garlic coarsely. Mix with rice. Sauté mushrooms with a little more garlic and add to rice. Add olive oil to rice and mix well. Place in casserole dish, shred goat cheese on top and bake for 30 minutes at 350° F. Garnish with yellow dock seeds, mustard seeds and wild flowers. Serve on a bed of leafy greens. Serves 10–12. Eat with a loved one and give thanks!

PURSLANE

—Terra Reneau

KASHI AND BROCCOLI CASSEROLE

1 cup kashi, cooked
1 cup basmati rice, cooked
1 onion, chopped
1 stalk celery, chopped
1 Tbsp. olive oil
2 Tbsp. sesame seeds
Handful pumpkin seeds
6–8 chopped almonds

1 broccoli stalk with a small part
    of the stem, steamed and
    chopped
Rice mozzarella cheese
Tofu American cheese
Handful of violet flowers or rose
    petals

Once you have the kashi and basmati grains cooked, set them aside to drain. Sauté the onion and celery in oil for 5 minutes or until clear and slightly browned. Add the sesame seeds, pumpkin seeds and chopped almonds. Continue to sauté. When onion/celery/seed mix is ready add the cooked kashi, rice and broccoli and toss gently. Grease a baking dish. Put in ½ of the broccoli/kashi mix and spread out in a layer. Add 2–3 slices of rice mozzarella cheese. Put the rest of the broccoli/kashi mix on top, spread out and lay 2–3 slices of tofu American cheese on top. Put it in the oven to melt the cheese (10 minutes at 400° F). Top with edible flowers and serve warm or bring to a potluck supper and serve at room temperature. Serves 8 as a side dish.

—Sharon Murphy

FAR EASTERN VEGETABLE BAKE

2 tsp. oil
1 sliced onion
2 tsp. crushed garlic
1½ Tbsp. ground cumin
1½ tsp. ground cinnamon
14 oz. can of tomatoes in juice
5 cups chopped fresh vegetables,
　　e.g. sweet potato, broccoli,

carrot, cauliflower, parsnip,
　celery
1 grated white potato

Topping
1 cup *crème fraiche* or sour
　cream
2–3 Tbsp. grated Parmesan

Heat oil in ovenproof casserole, add onion, and sauté until soft but not colored. Add the garlic and spices and cook for another minute. Add tomatoes and vegetables and stir to combine. Simmer for 25 minutes over low heat. Spread crème fraiche or sour cream and Parmesan over top and grill for 5–10 minutes until golden brown. Serves 3–4.

—JANE CARDIN

Salt Substitute

Mix together equal parts of the following dried herbs or any other ed-ible wild greens:

Comfrey	Chives
Nettle	Dandelion leaf
Plantain	Sourgrass
Lovage	Onion greens

Small amounts of any of the following can also be added:

Basil
Dill
Oregano
Garlic greens
Thyme

Chop and dry the herbs in a well-ventilated area, away from direct sunlight. They can be dried in an oven that has been heated to 200–250° F and then turned off. Be sure to watch them so they do not burn.

Combine the dried herbs together in a blender or food processor. You can add a little sea salt if you like, but then it isn't a salt substitute any more! Store in an airtight container away from heat and light.

—JULIE MANCHESTER, WOODSONG HERBALS

BURDOCK BLOOM SPIKE BAKE

4 cups cooked burdock bloom
   spike rounds
1 cup Parmesan cheese
⅔ cup bread crumbs
⅓ cup mayonnaise

2 Tbsp. vegetable oil
½ cup finely chopped onions
2 cloves garlic, minced
Paprika

Collect at least a dozen burdock bloom spikes (flower stalks) when they
are about 1–2 feet high and still in the process of growing taller (way before the flowers show up). Burdock is usually at this stage in the Boston
area during the first two weeks in June. Cut them as close to the ground as
you can and strip off the large leaves and stalks. When you get the bloom
spikes home, peel off the outer rind, which tends to be stringy and bitter.
Chop the peeled bloom spikes into rounds about ⅓ inch thick. Drop the
spikes into an ample supply of boiling salted water and boil until tender
(10–15 minutes). Remove and drain. Add all ingredients except the paprika to 4 cups of the boiled burdock bloom spikes and combine. Spread
in a pie pan or flat baking dish and sprinkle paprika over the top. Bake at
350° F until bubbly (about 20 minutes). Serve hot with crackers. Serves 6–8.

—Russ Cohen

15-MINUTE HERBAL FISH

Cleaned fish
5 lemon verbena leaves, chopped
5 lemon balm leaves, chopped
1 large slice fresh tomato, sprinkled with grated cheese

Place cleaned fish on heavy-duty aluminum foil. Top with the leaves,
tomato and cheese; pinch edges of foil together to wrap fish up and grill
until done.

—Andrea Rogers

A Special Marinade

I use this marinade for cooking chicken, but it can be used for veggie dishes too. Mix together a little of the following ingredients: water, tamari, vinegar (your choice), mustard powder, fresh sliced garlic, fresh grated ginger, sunflower seed oil, sage oil, hawthorn flower and/or berry brandy, crumbled kelp and salt. Pour over and through a whole chicken before slow-baking it at 350° F for 1½ hours.

There are infinite varieties possible with this marinade. It never comes out the same way twice and is always great! I sometimes add toasted sesame oil and a little hot pepper sesame oil instead of the sage and sunflower seed oils.

—ROBIN ROSE BENNETT, WISEWOMAN HEALING WAYS

TOM'S WORLD-FAMOUS CHICKEN RECIPE

This recipe got its name on a dare. After many years of experimenting with my herbal vinegar, my husband came up with this awesome herbal combination. After several years of friends and family begging him to make "his chicken," I asked him to package the blend and sell it in conjunction with my herbal vinegar at some of the craft shows that we do. We went back and forth with names for about a week. The blend had to have a name before a Sunday craft show. On Saturday, I just told Tom: "I'm gonna name it Tom's World-famous Chicken. *"You wouldn't do that," he said (with a smile of pride on his face). "Yep! That's the name!" I said. "No! You wouldn't dare," Tom said. We dropped the subject, and the next day I went to the show with samples of* Tom's World-famous Chicken Blend. *When I got home Tom was shocked that we had sold out on the first day.*

1½ lb. boneless skinless chicken breast	2 tsp. dried basil
½ cup butter	½ tsp. each salt, pepper and paprika
½ clove garlic, crushed	¼ tsp. nutmeg
1 Tbsp. herbal vinegar* (your choice)	

Pierce chicken several times prior to cooking to absorb flavor. Melt butter in large skillet. Add all other ingredients except the chicken and bring to a boil slowly. Add chicken and bring to a boil again. Reduce heat, cover and simmer 20–25 minutes, turning chicken several times. Serve over rice or pasta. Makes 4 servings.

Time-saving method: Melt butter in microwave. Put melted butter and all ingredients in a glass baking dish. Bake at 325° for 20–25 minutes, turning chicken once.

—MICHELLE AND TOM LAWRENSON, HERBAL HARVEST

*See page 62 for how to make vinegars.

HERBED CHICKEN

2½ lbs. chicken, cut up
4 Tbsp. Epicurean Delights Lemon Pepper*
1 cup lemon juice
½ clove garlic, minced

Salt and pepper chicken. Coat with lemon juice. Sprinkle lemon pepper on all sides. Place chicken in a glass baking dish, pour remaining lemon juice over chicken, and place minced garlic on and around chicken. Bake at 350°F for 1 hour or until tender. Baste occasionally with drippings. Serves 4.

—Allie Letson, The Potted Herb

WILD SPIEDIES (KEBOBS)

1 lb. cubed venison (or other wild meat)
¼ cup olive oil
⅛ cup red wine or herb vinegar
⅛ cup soy sauce
½ tsp. each dried oregano and marjoram
2 Tbsp. ketchup
3 cloves wild garlic, minced

Combine ingredients and place in a container with an airtight lid. Marinate 3–5 days in the refrigerator. When ready to cook the spiedies, skewer the meat and cook over hot coals. Serve on Italian rolls. Serves 4.

—Sheryl Allyn, Wilderness Way School

*Epicurean Delights Lemon Pepper is available via mail order from the *Potted Herb* (see page 230) and contains lemon juice powder, parsley, garlic and onion powder and fresh black pepper.

Marinade for Venison or Elk

¼ cup olive oil
⅛ cup red wine vinegar
⅛ cup tamari
1 Tbsp. Worcestershire sauce
1-inch piece fresh ginger root,
   grated

Pinch cayenne
2 cloves raw garlic, minced
½ tsp. salt
Freshly ground black pepper

Marinate game for 4 to 8 hours and cook as desired. We like to use it on kebobs. Makes ½ cup.

—GREG WULFF-TILFORD, ANIMALS APAWTHECARY

WILD CROCKPOT STEW

½ cup wheat flour
1 tsp. sweet basil
½ tsp. each dried parsley flakes,
   oregano, ground spicebush
   berries (or allspice), salt and
   pepper
2 lbs. cubed venison (or other
   wild meat)

2 cans mushroom soup
1 cup water
3 celery stalks, sliced
2 carrots, sliced
1 onion, chopped
2 cloves wild garlic, minced

Combine flour, herbs, salt and pepper. Roll venison in flour mixture and brown in skillet. Place all ingredients into crockpot and cook on low overnight (8–10 hours). Serve over baked potatoes. Makes 4–6 servings

—SHERYL ALLYN, WILDERNESS WAY SCHOOL

MEAL IN A BUNDLE

3 lbs. lean chuck, cut into 1-inch cubes
1 cup chopped onions
½ cup chopped fresh parsley
3 Tbsp. fresh lovage
Salt and pepper to taste

8 medium potatoes, peeled and diced
8 carrots, cut into ¼-inch slices
½ Tbsp. chopped fresh thyme
2 10½-oz. cans golden mushroom soup
Worcestershire sauce

Mix all ingredients and divide into 12 equal portions. Place each portion on a 16-inch square of heavy-duty aluminum foil. Add a dash of Worcestershire sauce and 1 Tbs. of water to each portion. Season with salt and pepper. Bring up corners of foil and twist at top to close. Place bundles on grill 2 inches above grey hot coals. Let cook 1 hour and serve in foil. Serves 12.

—JUDITH GRAVES, LAMBS & THYME

MAMA'S MEAT BALLS

Mama is Peggy Hardee of Marion, South Carolina.

1 lb. lean ground beef
¼ cup grated onion
1 egg, beaten
Salt to taste
½ tsp. rosemary

Mix above ingredients well. Shape into 1-inch balls and place in glass baking dish. Cover and microwave 8–10 minutes on medium high or sauté in oil in a skillet on the stove top, turning to brown on all sides. Drain and serve with your favorite sauce. Makes 12–15 1½-inch meatballs.

—ALLIE LETSON, THE POTTED HERB

MEDITERRANEAN PORK CHOPS

1 tsp. vegetable oil
4 loin pork chops, ½" thick with fat removed
Salt
4 Tbsp. Epicurean Delights Mediterranean Herb Blend*
½ cup water

Place oil in a nonstick skillet over medium high heat. Salt pork chops to taste and sprinkle on the herb blend. Place pork chops in the skillet and add water to bottom of skillet. Cover tightly, reduce heat to low and simmer for 1 hour or until chops are tender. Serves 4

—ALLIE LETSON, THE POTTED HERB

Lemon & Herb Marinade

⅔ cup lemon juice
⅓ cup olive oil
1 tsp. each salt and sugar
1½ tsp. tarragon

Combine all ingredients in a bowl and stir. Marinate for 1–2 hours. This is great with chicken wings and pork chops.

—ALLIE LETSON. THE POTTED HERB

*Epicurean Delights Mediterranean Herb Blend is available by mail order from The Potted Herb and contains oregano, rosemary, marjoram, thyme, sage, savory and parsley.

QUICK QUICHE

Unbaked pie crust
10 oz. chopped steamed spinach, well-drained
2 cups cheddar cheese

5 fresh eggs
2 cups milk
1 Tbsp. fresh parsley, chopped
Dash of salt and pepper

Place spinach in the pie crust. Mix all other ingredients together. Pour liquid mixture over the spinach. Bake in preheated 350°F oven for 45 minutes or until the top is browned. Serves 4–6.

—KATHLEEN O'MARA. THE HERB NETWORK

Cooking Dandelion Greens

Dandelion greens can be sautéed, steamed, boiled or eaten raw. The less you cook them, the more nutrients they will have. The healthiest way to eat them is raw or steamed. But if eating bitter wild greens is new to you, the best way to cook them is to boil them in two or more changes of water. Harvest the tenderest, youngest leaves, filling your colander more than full (for 2 servings). Wash and place in a stainless steel pot. Cover with boiling water. Bring back to a boil. Strain off the water and cover with more boiling water, repeating the process 2–3 times. If the greens need more cooking, add a small amount of boiling water and steam until tender.

SUNSHINE QUICHE

A wonderful dish that requires a bit of prep time. Be sure to start early. You can always make it ahead and warm it in the oven before serving.

Tart shell:
6 Tbsp. very cold butter
1 cup flour
1 egg yolk
2 Tbsp. water
Filling:
3 cups fresh dandelion greens
2 small onions, chopped
oil

Soft butter to grease cooking
  dish or pan
2 cups dandelion flowers
1 11-oz. can corn
2 portabello (or any other)
  mushrooms
4 eggs
2 cups cream or half & half
Nutmeg

To make the shell, cut the butter into slices and add the flour. Blend with fingers until crumbly. In a separate bowl, combine the egg yolk with the water and whisk. Add this to the dry mixture, knead and work into a ball. Wrap in plastic wrap and refrigerate for ½ hour.

Meanwhile, wash and cook the dandelion greens. They should cook down to about 1¼ cups. Chop the onions. (To avoid the tears caused by onions, light a small candle before you start chopping; it works every time!) Sauté the onions in oil until they are soft and golden.

Preheat the oven to 425° F and butter the bottom of a 9-inch casserole dish or springform pan. Remove the dough from the refrigerator and roll out. Gently pat into the dish, and trim off the edges. Be sure to save the extra dough.

Remove the stems of the dandelion blossoms and add to a large bowl. Chop up the cooked greens and add them to the bowl along with the onions, corn and mushrooms. Blend well and spoon into the shell. Combine the 4 eggs, cream and a pinch of nutmeg and pour over the filling.

If you wish to decorate the top with the extra dough, now is the time. Simply roll out the dough and make shapes with a knife. I use a little crescent moon; it adds a little magic to the dish. Place decoration on top of filling and bake for 15 minutes. Lower the heat to 350° F and bake for ½ hour more. Exact cooking time may vary depending on your oven; to test, insert a knife into the filling; if it comes out clean quiche is done. You will find this dish is well worth the time you put into it.

—Rachel Schneider, Flower Power Herbals

SMOKED SALMON-NETTLE FRITATTA

This is a good spring dish. We raise our own chickens, so we tend to eat a lot of eggs. Moreover, we have woods filled with carpets of stinging nettles. My brother is a fisherman, so smoked salmon is also abundant in our house.

8 eggs
2 Tbsp. fresh French thyme,
    sweet basil or cinnamon basil
Salt and pepper to taste
2 Tbsp. olive oil
⅓ cup green onions, chopped

1 sweet red pepper, chopped
1 cup cooked/drained nettles
4 oz. smoked salmon, sliced in
    ½-inch pieces
2 oz. feta cheese, crumbled

Preheat oven to 375° F. Whip the eggs with the herbs and seasonings. Heat the oil over medium heat in a 12-inch iron skillet. Add onions, red pepper and cooked nettles. Sauté until vegetables are soft (approximately 5 minutes). Lower the heat and add the egg and herb mixture. Stir 2–3 times. Sprinkle crumbled salmon and feta cheese on top. Put whole frying pan into the oven and bake for 8–12 minutes until the fritatta puffs slightly. Cut into wedges and serve. Serves 4.

STUFFED MUSHROOMS

This is excellent as a main course for a vegetarian dinner or as an appetizer or hors d'oeuvre at a more elaborate meal. The mushrooms can be made ahead of time, refrigerated and warmed up when needed. As an appetizer, use the baby mushrooms; as a main course use the larger ones.

6–10 mushrooms per person, cleaned
1 clove garlic per person, chopped
Olive oil
Butter
1 onion, chopped
1 handful almonds or nuts, chopped
½ cup dried currants
Parsley, minced
Heart's Delight Herbs*
Dash of hot sauce
Hard cheese, grated

Spoon out or break off the stems of the mushrooms. Sauté mushroom caps and garlic in a mixture of olive oil and butter until barely tender. Remove mushroom caps to a baking pan, and set aside to cool, cap side down, cavity up. Reserve oil and pan juices in skillet. Chop the mushroom stems and mix with the onion, nuts, currants, parsley, herbs and hot sauce; put mixture through the coarse grind of a blender. Sauté lightly in the leftover oil and mushroom juices in skillet in which the caps were cooked. Let cool, then place a teaspoon of mixture inside each mushroom cap. Sprinkle with grated cheese and bake in a 350° F oven until the cheese is hot and bubbling. Serve garnished with parsley.

—Jeanne Rose

*Heart's Delight Herbs (a salt substitute): 1 part each basil, chervil, lovage, oregano, parsley, rosemary, savory, thyme, tarragon.

Simple Wild Mushroom Treats

I live in an oak forest nestled in the hills of Western Massachusetts. I love to go mushrooming along the old logging roads, basket over my arm and my cat Cerridwen for company.

Chicken Mushroom (*Polyporus sulphureus*). This large, orange fungus grows in layers out of old tree stumps. It is named for its delicate chicken-like flavor. A simple and delicious way to prepare it is to slice it and sauté it lightly in butter. Spoon the sautéed mushrooms onto rice and top with fresh chopped parsley.

Horn of Plenty (*Craterellus cornucopioides*). These dark brown silky mushrooms are thin and delicate and shaped like little hollow trumpets on the forest floor. If you are lucky enough to find a few, look around; there will generally be a few patches scattered about nearby. I like to sauté them gently and then add them to a cheese omelette. Be careful to cook mushrooms separately from the eggs, or the eggs will take on a dark brown tinge. Use a delicate cheese to prevent masking the flavor of the mushrooms.

Oyster Mushroom (*Pleurotus ostreatus*). These grow inside and around old decayed trees. They are excellent sautéed with sliced onions and served over brown rice that has been cooked with a hint of garlic. Add tamari at the end.

Caution: Do not eat any wild mushroom unless absolutely positive of its identification. See page 12 for more information.

—ELLEN EVERT HOPMAN

NETTLE PIE

In many European countries nettles* are considered a delicacy. They are also highly nutritious.

Pie pastry or pizza dough rolled
  out to a 12-inch round
1 small leek, sliced
3 cloves garlic, minced
1 Tbsp. olive oil
1–1½ lbs. fresh nettle tips, or
  nettles mixed with other
  greens

1 Tbsp. dried basil or pesto
¼–½ cup grated Parmesan or ½
  lb. feta cheese or firm tofu,
  crumbled

In a cast iron skillet sauté garlic and leek in oil over medium heat until soft. Lower heat and add nettles and basil. Stir. Cook until greens are wilted. Remove from heat. Add cheese or tofu. Place dough on a baking sheet. Cover half the dough with the nettle mixture, leaving about ½ inch at the edge. Fold the other half of the dough over, completely covering the greens. Seal the edges. Prick the top of the dough with a fork. Place in a 350° F oven and bake until golden brown, about 30–45 minutes. Serves 2–4.

—Colette Gardiner

*For more about nettles and how to harvest them, see page 50.

WILD GREEN BURRITOS

1 medium onion, chopped
3 cloves garlic, chopped
2 Tbsp. sesame oil
5 cups wild greens, chopped
   (dandelions, lamb's quarters,
   amaranth)

½ cup sour cream
6 flour tortillas
2 cups grated cheddar cheese

Sauté onions and garlic in hot sesame oil. Lower heat and add greens. Cook on low heat 10–15 minutes, until leaves are wilted. Stir in sour cream. Heat tortillas one at a time on a grill or nonstick skillet. Fill each tortilla with a large spoonful of cooked greens. Sprinkle with grated cheese. Fold in one end of tortilla and roll. Serve.

—Vickie Shufer

WILD EGGROLLS

These are a wonderful treat in spring or summer!

Wild greens—collect whatever is available, for example: violet leaves, chives, mustard greens, salad burnet, sheep or French sorrel, red clover leaves, dandelion leaves, lovage, yellow dock leaves, nettles, watercress
1 onion, chopped
2–3 cloves garlic, chopped
Mushrooms, chopped (shiitakes are especially good)

olive oil for sautéing and deep frying
1 lb. tofu, cut in small cubes
1 large grated carrot
1 handful hijiki or arame, soaked in water
Fresh or dried ginger root, grated
1–2 Tbsp. tamari
1 Tbsp. toasted sesame oil
1 package eggroll wrappers

Sauté onion, garlic and mushrooms in 1–2 Tbs. oil. Add tofu and carrot. Continue to sauté a few more minutes. Add seaweed, ginger, tamari and sesame oil. Stir well. Add washed, chopped greens and stir. Gently simmer till they are wilted. Fill eggroll wrappers according to directions. Place in well-heated oil (it will sizzle when you add a few drops of water) and deep fry until lightly brown. Do a few at a time in a large pot. Drain on paper towels or a paper bag immediately. Serve with little bowls of hot mustard, tamari, or sweet and sour sauce and some long-grain brown rice. Serves 10.

—Jane Smolnik

WILD GREENS SPANIKOPITA

1 cup wild or regular onion
2 Tbsp. olive oil
3 cups wild greens, well washed
(lamb's quarters, galinsoga,
chickweed or other mild
greens; stronger greens such
as field mustard can be added
or substituted for a stronger
bite, but you may want to parboil them a few minutes first.)

1 cup feta cheese (or substitute
ricotta or cottage)
2 eggs
2 Tbsp. each fresh parsley and
wild chives, chopped
Salt and pepper to taste
12 phyllo pastry leaves
¼ cup melted butter

Sauté onions in the oil and add the greens; cover and cook 5 minutes or until the greens are wilted and tender. Add cheese, eggs, parsley, wild chives, salt and pepper; mix in well, and cool slightly. Cut phyllo leaves to make 24 sheets; layer the first 12 sheets in a well-greased oblong baking dish (6" x 10" or equivalent), brushing each layer with the melted butter. Spoon the cooked greens/cheese/mixture into the baking dish and spread evenly over the phyllo. Cover with the remaining phyllo, brushing each layer with butter as before. Bake at 350° F for 1 hour or until golden. Serves 6–8.

—RUSS COHEN

DESSERTS

Herbalists have a reputation for being strict health nuts. One look through this section will undoubtedly demolish that reputation. Enjoy!

TAYLOR'S TARRAGON WAFERS

½ cup butter
½ cup brown sugar, firmly
   packed
1 tsp. vanilla
1 egg, beaten
½ cup toasted sesame seeds

½ cup crushed nuts
1½ tsp. dried tarragon
¾ cup white flour
¼ tsp. baking powder
¼ tsp. salt

Cream butter, sugar and vanilla together. Beat in egg, stir in sesame seeds, nuts and tarragon. Sift dry ingredients together and add to mix. Drop in small mounds about 3 inches apart onto greased baking sheet. Bake at 350° F for 8–10 minutes. Cool before removing from sheet. Makes about 2 dozen.

—MARY ELLEN ROSS

Buying Lavender Blossoms

The lavender blossoms sold in stores are generally not for consumption. They include additives used for maintaining their smell. Be sure that the lavender you use for food or medicine does not contain these additives. Instead, your own unsprayed garden lavender would be perfect. Lavender's most common use is in potpourri.

LAVENDER SHORTBREAD COOKIES

¼ cup confectioner's sugar
9 Tbsp. butter
1½ cups flour
2 Tbsp. fresh lavender blossoms
1 Tbsp. granulated sugar

Mix confectioner's sugar and butter. Add flour and lavender. Knead until soft. Roll out to ⅜-inch thick. Cut in rounds. Bake at 350° F until light golden. Sprinkle tops with sugar. Makes about 2 dozen.

—Susan Wittig Albert, reprinted with permission from *Thyme and Seasons Herbal Teas*

Cilantro/Coriander
(Coriandrum sativum)

Confusing but true, these are the same plant. Cilantro is the leaf and coriander is the seed. The seeds are used in everything from stews to pastries and are an ingredient in curry powder. The leaves are the main seasoning in many Chinese, Mexican and Mediterranean dishes.

The seed is known for its ability to rid the digestive system of wind, ease stomach cramps and diarrhea, especially in children. It also stimulates the appetite. It can be used instead of dill to make "gripe water" (an old remedy for colic). Bruise a teaspoon of seeds, put into a small saucepan and pour a cup of boiling water over them. Cover and let steep for 5 minutes. Give to children by the teaspoonful and to adults by the cup before meals.

CORIANDER CRISPS

1 cup shortening
⅔ cup sugar
2 eggs
1½ cups flour

1 tsp. each ground coriander and lemon extract
1 Tbsp. crushed coriander seed

Cream shortening and sugar. Add eggs, beating well. Gradually add flour, ground coriander and lemon extract. Beat until blended. Drop 2 inches apart on an ungreased cookie sheet. Flatten with bottom of a glass that has been dipped in water. Sprinkle with coriander seeds. Bake at 375° F for 6–8 minutes. Cool on rack. Makes 2 dozen.

—SUSAN WITTIG ALBERT, REPRINTED WITH PERMISSION FROM *THYME AND SEASONS HERBAL TEAS*

ROSE HIP COOKIES

These cookies are wonderful as Valentine treats. They are always a hit at herb classes, too.

½ cup butter	1 pinch nutmeg
½ cup sugar	1 tsp. rosehips
1 egg, beaten	1⅓ cups flour
½ tsp. rosewater	Confectioner's sugar

Cream butter and sugar; add beaten egg, salt, rosewater and nutmeg. Put rose hips in a blender and chop for one minute or until they are in ⅛-inch pieces. Blend flour and rose hips into egg mixture and mix well. Drop batter by spoonfuls onto a cookie sheet. Bake at 375° F for 10–15 minutes. Remove cookies from sheet and roll in confectioner's sugar. Makes 24 cookies.

—PENNY KING

Rose Hip Honey

Fill a quart jar with freshly picked rose hips. Bring some water to a boil and pour the water over them. Cover and let steep overnight. The hips should be mushy; if not, cook gently over low heat until they are. Press the hips and water through a coarse sieve or chinois and measure. Add an equal amount of honey to this purée. Store in the refrigerator. Use as soon as possible.

—JEANNE ROSE

GINGER CRISPS

These cookies are equally as popular with kids as with adults. You can cut the cookies in simple round shapes or ones that best express your mood.

2½ cups unbleached white flour
2½ cups whole wheat flour
½ tsp. baking soda
1 cup softened butter
½ cup packed brown sugar
⅓ cup each maple syrup and
  honey

1 tsp. each grated lemon rind
  and vanilla extract
1 tsp. ground cinnamon
3 Tbsp. grated fresh ginger (or
  1½ tsp. ground)

Combine the flours and baking soda in a medium-sized bowl. Beat the sugar and butter in a separate bowl until creamy. Add the syrup, honey, lemon rind and vanilla and blend well. Add the cinnamon and ginger and mix again. Gradually add the flour mixture and mix well until a soft dough is formed. Press dough to ½-inch thick on waxed paper. Cover and chill for at least 2 hours. The longer it is chilled, the easier it will be to handle. Using small portions of the dough at one time, returning the remaining dough to the refrigerator, roll dough to ⅛-inch thickness and cut into desired shapes, on a lightly floured surface, using a well-floured rolling pin. Bake the cookies on a greased baking sheet for 8–10 minutes at 350° F. Repeat the process with the remaining dough. Makes 6–8 dozen. Refrigerate any leftover pieces of dough until needed.

—KARYN SIEGAL-MAIER

Aphrodisiac Honey

Briskly rub about ¾–1 cup of dried rose petals/blossoms between your hands, crumbling them almost to powder. Do the same with ¾–1 cup of dried bitter orange blossoms. Pour 1 quart of clover blossom honey into a saucepan. Add the pulverized flowers and stir.

Grate in fresh ginger to taste, or approximately 2 inches of root. Cook on lowest heat for about 30–40 minutes, stirring frequently. Pour mixture, unstrained, back into the honey jar. Enjoy by the spoonful. Feed it to your lover or add to any recipe that calls for honey. Yum! Gently stimulating.

—Robin Rose Bennett

SAFFRON-CURRANT REFRIGERATOR COOKIES

½ tsp. saffron threads, broken
2 Tbsp. boiling water
1 cup softened butter
1 cup sugar
1 egg

2½ cups unbleached white flour
½ tsp. baking powder
⅛ tsp. salt
½ cup currants

Soak the saffron in the boiling water. Cream the butter and sugar together. Beat in the egg. Add the saffron/water mixture. Sift the flour, baking powder and salt in a large mixing bowl. Add the flour mixture to the wet ingredients, ½ cup at a time, until a soft dough forms. Fold in the currants. Refrigerate the cookie dough until quite firm, about 2 hours. Shape into small balls and flatten with a fork, or the palm of your hand, into ½-inch rounds. Place unused dough in the refrigerator until ready to use. Bake on an ungreased cookie sheet in a preheated 375° F oven for 8–10 minutes. Makes 4 dozen.

—Karyn Siegal-Maier

Herbal Tea Party

One of my favorite workshops is called "Herbal Serendipity," which I bill as a play day. The most popular activity that day is to adorn ourselves with plant materials. We make crowns of lady's mantle leaves, using their sturdy stems to join them together; we put on false fingernails of fairy rose or phlox petals (just the right size!) and carry staffs of six-foot tall mullein plants. Then we sit down to feast on a fresh wild salad and tea. If you fold a lady's mantle leaf into a cone shape, it will serve as a cup. Iced tea poured into these looks like liquid gold, and water looks like quicksilver. It is spectacular fun for children of all ages!

—Tina Finneyfrock

THUMBPRINT COOKIES

½ cup soft butter
¼ cup light brown sugar
1 large egg, separated
½ tsp. vanilla extract
1 cup flour
1 pinch salt

1 cup or more hickory nuts, finely chopped (or walnuts black or regular)
⅓ cup sparkling crabapple or barberry jelly

Mix butter, brown sugar, egg yolk and vanilla extract together thoroughly. Add flour and salt gradually. Mix the dough until dry spots disappear. Preheat oven to 375° F. Wet hands and roll dough into balls 1 inch in diameter. Dip each ball into slightly beaten egg white and roll into chopped nuts. Place about 1 inch apart on an ungreased cookie sheet. Bake 5 minutes and take out of the oven. Press thumb gently into the center of each cookie to make a depression. Put back into the oven and bake for 8 minutes more. Check to make sure depressions are still there; if not, press thumb in again. Set out awhile to cool; then place a small lump of jelly in the center of each cookie. Makes about 15 cookies.

—Russ Cohen

ANISE DESSERT BARS

These bars are simply delicious, wonderful with tea or champagne.

For crust:
½ cup softened butter
1⅓ cups flour
¼ cup sugar
For filling:
2 eggs

¾ cup sugar
2 Tbsp. flour
¼ tsp. baking powder
3 Tbsp. fresh lemon juice
1 Tbsp. finely chopped fresh
    anise hyssop flowers

Preheat oven to 350° F. Combine all the ingredients for the crust in a mixing bowl and mix until smooth. Spread the batter in a lightly greased 9-inch pan and bake until edges are lightly browned (15–20 minutes). While the crust is baking, blend together all the ingredients for the filling. Pour over the crust and bake another 20 minutes, until the filling is set. Cool. Cut in squares and serve.

—Rachel Schneider, Flower Power Herbals

CANDIED ANGELICA

Select young stems and stalks of angelica. Cut into 4- or 5-inch lengths, place in a glass or crockery vessel and pour over them 2 cups boiling water mixed with ½ cup salt. Cover and leave for 24 hours. Lift out angelica, drain on a wire drainer, peel off stringy bits and wash in cold water. Make a syrup of 1½ pounds sugar and 1½ pints water, and boil for 10 minutes. Place the angelica in the boiling syrup for 20 minutes. Lift out and drain for 4 days on a wire drainer.

Boil again for 10–20 minutes in the same syrup. If you end up with "barley sugar" (which I do frequently), it makes a very pleasant boiled sweet for Easter! Allow to cool in the syrup, lift out and drain for 3 or 4 days. Strew well with sugar and store in airtight jars.

—Caroline Holmes

Crystallizing

This is a decorative and delicious way to preserve edible flowers and small leaves, e.g. borage, rose petals, lavender or mint.

3 parts gum arabic or acacia powder
4 parts rosewater
Super-fine granulated sugar

Dissolve the gum arabic in the rosewater, stirring gently until fully blended. Coat the flowers and leaves on all sides using a paintbrush and gently sift sugar over them. Leave to dry in a shady, dry, warm spot on a sheet of grease-proof or parchment paper. Store in an airtight container. Serve as a garnish for desserts or with coffee.

—CAROLINE HOLMES

FRUIT FIX

1 lb. pitted dates
1 lb. dried figs
1 lb. pitted prunes
1½ lbs. raisins
2–4 Tbsp. rose hip powder

Simmer the fruits together in 8–10 cups water. When soft, mash together (or put in food processor) and add the rose hip powder. Use this calcium-rich, estrogen-enhancing spread in place of jams and jellies. Try it on a whole wheat cracker when you think you want a cookie. To relieve constipation, cook in prune juice instead of water. Makes about 2 quarts.

—SUSUN WEED, REPRINTED WITH PERMISSION
FROM *THE MENOPAUSAL YEARS: THE WISE WOMAN WAY*

SWEET LAVENDER ORANGES

6 large seedless oranges
1 cup raw sugar
1 cup water
1 Tbsp. chopped fresh lavender flowers
3 Tbsp. Grand Marnier (optional)

Slice the oranges into fine rounds, peel off the skins and set the fruit in serving bowls. Take the finely sliced orange peel (no white parts) and boil with the sugar, water and lavender. Boil to a syrup. Cool. Add liqueur, if you wish. Pour the syrup over the fruit, chill and garnish with fresh lavender flowers. Serves 6.

—Jane Carden

PECONIC RIVER HERB FARM LEMON VERBENA PEACHES

1 8-oz. package neufchâtel
   cheese, softened
¼ cup honey
½ cup lemon verbena leaves,
   washed and spun dry

4 fresh peaches
½ lemon, squeezed
Lemon verbena leaves for garnish

Process cheese, honey and lemon verbena leaves in food processor until smooth. Wash peaches and cut in half. Dip peach halves in lemon juice. Spoon about 3 tablespoons of cheese mixture on cut side of peach half. Place lemon verbena garnish on each peach as if it is the stem. Serve immediately. Cheese spread can be made one day ahead. Serves 8.

—Jill Yeck, Peconic River Herb Farm

ELDERBERRY TART

Pastry Crust (see pages 186 and 187 for recipes)
2 cups fresh berries (elderberries, huckleberries, salal or blackberries), cleaned
2 Tbsp. arrowroot powder
3–4 Tbsp. pure maple syrup

Spread the berries over the crust. Mix arrowroot into the maple syrup. Drizzle over the berries. Bake at 375° F for 10 minutes, then lower to 350° F for 35–50 minutes. Serves 4–6.

—JO JENNER

Elderberry

The elderberry bush grows in abundance in New England and is a favorite for many reasons. I use the berries to make a delicious cough syrup, which also helps heal colds and flu. The berries keep well in the freezer for over a year although they are generally used up by spring! They can also be made into pies, jellies and wine. Elder flowers, which bloom in the spring, are also valuable. Dried, they are the basis of an ancient gypsy fever and cold tea. Combine equal parts dried elder flowers, peppermint and yarrow leaves. Steep 1 oz. of the mixture in a quart of boiling water for 15 minutes. Strain, reheat if necessary, drink 1 or 2 cups as hot as possible and get into bed. This diaphoretic formula will help you sweat out a cold or fever.

BANANA NO-CREAM PIE

2–3 ripe bananas
2 tsp. vanilla
1 Tbsp. lemon juice
½ cup oil
⅓ cup sugar
¼ tsp. salt

2½ cups tofu
3–4 sprigs fresh lemon verbena
    or lemon balm (reserve some
    leaves for garnish)
1 graham cracker crust

Blend everything (except the crust, of course!) in a blender until smooth. Save a few lemon verbena leaves for garnish. Pour into graham cracker crust and chill for 2–3 hours. Decorate with banana slices and lemon verbena or balm leaves. Serves 6.

—RISA MORNIS

Whole Wheat No-butter Crust

2 cups whole wheat pastry flour
½ tsp. salt
½ cup canola oil
¼ cup cold water

Mix the flour and salt together in a bowl. Add the oil and water to the flour. Stir immediately, but do not overmix. Roll dough between 2 pieces of plastic or pastry cloth. Invert the rolled crust into a 10-inch tart pan. Trim edges.

—JO JENNER

IMPOSSIBLE CUSTARD PIE

½ cup plus 1 Tbsp. Bisquick
½ cup sugar
2 cups milk
1 tsp. vanilla
4 eggs

3 Tbsp. melted butter
Few grains of salt
Nutmeg
Garnish: whipped cream, mint
    leaves, pansies

Mix pie ingredients together in a blender and pour into a well-greased glass pie plate. Sprinkle top with nutmeg. Bake at 400° F for 25–30 minutes. Serve with whipped cream, pansies and mint leaves on top. Cut into 12 small wedges.

—JUDITH GRAVES, LAMBS & THYME

Pastry Crust

1 cup butter
1½ cups white flour
1½ cups whole wheat pastry
    flour

2 Tbsp. sugar
1 lemon, juiced, rind removed
    and reserved
½ cup cold water

Cut butter, flours, sugar and grated rind of the lemon together until it is the consistency of course corn meal. Mix the water with juice of the lemon. Combine the mixtures by sprinkling in the liquid ingredients, one tablespoon at a time, stirring with a fork just until the particles are moistened and stick together. Cover and chill the dough for 30 minutes. Pat into pan ¼-inch thick. Chill again. Bake with desired filling.

RHUBARB PIE WITH CICELY

3 cups chopped fresh rhubarb
3 Tbsp. flour
½ cup sugar or honey
1 tsp. cinnamon powder
1 cup chopped tender sweet cicely leaves

Mix all ingredients together in a large bowl. Pour into a prepared pie shell and bake at 375° F for 45 minutes. Serves 6.

—LINDA QUINTANA

Sweet Cicely

Sweet cicely (*Myrrhis odorata*) is a tall perennial with large, delicate, bright green foliage resembling parsley. Every part of the plant is edible: the leaves taste as if sugar had been sprinkled upon them, the seed fruit has a delicious nutty flavor, and the root has a sweet aniseed flavor. The leaves are sweet enough to be used in pastries and are also good brewed as tea. The leaves and seeds can be added to salads, fruits or desserts for a unique flavor. The root can be peeled, chopped and added raw to salads or steamed or cooked in an Oriental vegetable stir-fry. Sweet cicely is a natural sweetener for diabetics. Medicinally, it is considered a digestive tonic.

RHUBARB BREAD PUDDING

3 cups milk
4 eggs, slightly beaten
8 slices toast, cubed
2 cups sliced rhubarb

2 cups sugar
Garnish: whipped cream, edible
  flowers

Scald milk. Add eggs and mix well. Add toast cubes, rhubarb and sugar.
Mix and pour into buttered 3-quart casserole. Bake at 350° F for 1 hour.
Serve with whipped cream and edible flowers. Serves 6–8.

—JUDITH GRAVES, LAMBS & THYME

Vanilla-scented Sugar

Split one fresh vanilla bean down the middle. Tuck both halves into a
large glass jar filled with white or natural cane sugar. Seal the jar and
shake occasionally. Within a week the sugar will pick up the aromatic
vanilla scent. The vanilla beans can remain in the sugar jar and/or be
reused as long as they are still fragrant.

—SHARLEEN ANDREWS-MILLER

ELDER BLOSSOM PUDDING

1 handful elder flowers, stems removed
4 thick slices stale bread, cut up
1 egg
Sugar, to taste
Milk

Mix the elder flowers with the cut-up bread and egg. Add sugar to taste, and enough milk to cover the pudding. Cook until the flowers soften and blend their tangy taste into the bread. The Gypsies often added a few tansy flowers to color the pudding yellow, but they have a rather bitter taste. Serves 4.

—JULIETTE DE BAIRACLI LEVY, REPRINTED WITH PERMISSION
FROM *NATURE'S CHILDREN*.

Elder Flower

The flower from the magical elder tree is a gentle decongestant for babies, children and adults. It is good for treating colds, coughs, fevers and influenza. It is a sweet-tasting flower that has been used since Elizabethan times in syrups, conserves and cosmetics. It is one of the ingredients in the well-known Gypsy Fever Formula (see page 185).

DANDY RHUBARB CRISP

This delicious crisp was created by Katie Sleutz, an 11-year-old, who took second place in the 1997 National Dandelion Cookoff's Amateur Division finals.

4 cups fresh rhubarb (cut)	¾ cup flour
1 cup dandelion petals	1 tsp. cinnamon
½ tsp. salt	⅓ cup butter
1½ cups sugar	

Heat oven to 350° F. Mix together rhubarb and dandelion petals. Place in an ungreased 10- x 6-inch baking dish. Sprinkle with salt. In separate bowl, mix together sugar, flour and cinnamon. Add butter to mixture and work together with pastry knife until crumbly. Sprinkle evenly over rhubarb and dandelions. Bake for 45 minutes or until topping is golden brown. Serve warm with light cream or ice cream. Serves 4–6.

—PETER GAIL, REPRINTED WITH PERMISSION FROM *THE GREAT DANDELION COOKBOOK.*

FENNEL CAKE WITH LAVENDER FROSTING

This herbal cake is not only easy to digest but can induce sleepiness as well, therefore making a most satisfying dessert.

2 cups raw fennel, bulb or greens
1 cup butter
1½ cups honey
1 cup raisins
2 cups water
2 tsp. cinnamon
2 tsp. nutmeg
1 tsp. cloves
4 cups whole wheat pastry flour
4 tsp. baking soda

1 cup chopped walnuts
Frosting:
1 lb. cream cheese or tofu
½ cup butter
½ cup honey
⅛ cup heavy cream or soy milk
1 tsp. vanilla extract
Grated rind of one lemon
2 Tbsp. dried lavender flowers,
    finely ground

Preheat oven to 325° F and grease two round 9-inch cake pans. Grate fennel bulb or chop fennel greens until fine. Place in a saucepan along with butter, honey, raisins, water and spices and bring to a boil; stir, then let simmer for 5 minutes. Mix flour, baking soda and nuts in a large bowl then add the simmered mixture and stir gently until all ingredients are blended. Pour cake batter evenly into cake pans and bake for 40 minutes or until golden brown. Cool for at least 10 minutes before popping cakes out of pans and setting on a cooling rack until room temperature, about 45 minutes.

For the frosting, mix together, preferably with a beater, cream cheese or tofu, butter, honey, cream or soy milk and vanilla extract. Whip in lemon rind and lavender. Frost the top of one cooled fennel cake. Place second cake on top and use remaining frosting to cover the top and sides. Garnish with a fresh fennel leaf or lavender sprig. Serves 12.

—ANDREA MURRAY

SPICY APPLE CAKE

I have been making this cake for over 30 years. It is wonderful served warm with whipped cream.

2 cooking apples, peeled, cored and chopped	½ tsp. salt
¾ cup raw sugar	1 tsp. cinnamon
½ cup melted butter	½ tsp. each fresh grated nutmeg and allspice
1 large egg	1 cup raisins
1½ cups flour	¾ cup chopped walnuts
1 tsp. baking soda	Sifted confectioner's sugar

Preheat oven to 375°. Mix the apples with the sugar. Blend the butter and beaten egg and pour over the apples. Sift dry ingredients and add to apple mixture. Mix well, adding in raisins and walnuts. Grease a cake tin or deep flan tin and spread in mixture. Arrange some whole walnuts on top. Bake for 45–50 minutes. Turn out and lightly coat with sifted confectioner's sugar.

—JANE CARDEN

THE HEARTIEST CAKE

This cake is dairy-free, fat-free and sugar-free.

1 cup soy milk
½ cup applesauce
1 Tbsp. stevia (natural sweetener)*
4 tsp. baking powder
1 cup blue corn meal

1 cup 6-grain flour
1 tsp. each cinnamon, ginger, coriander, cardamom
½ cup raisins
½ cup sunflower seeds
Sesame seeds

Preheat oven to 425° F. Mix together the soy milk, applesauce and stevia until well blended. Add the baking powder and whisk until foamy. Add the corn meal, flour and spices and beat until smooth. Mix in the raisins and sunflower seeds. Put in an 8-inch round or 9-inch square pan. Cover with sesame seeds. Bake for 25 minutes.

—Mary Pat Palmer

CARAWAY CAKE

1 cup butter
1 cup sugar
2 eggs, well beaten
1 cup flour
1 tsp. baking powder

1 tsp. nutmeg
4 Tbsp. candied citrus peel
1 tsp. caraway seeds
¼ cup brandy

Cream the butter and sugar until smooth. Add eggs and mix well. Sift together the flour, baking powder and nutmeg. Gradually add the flour mixture and blend well. Fold in the candied peel, caraway seeds and just enough brandy to lend a moist consistency. Pour into a 9-inch bread pan. Bake for 1 hour or until the center is set, at 400° F. Serve warm with 2–3 tablespoons of brandy drizzled over the top.

—Karyn Siegal-Maier

*See page 42 for more about stevia.

Egg and Oil Substitute

Use 2 tablespoons of flaxseeds and 1 tablespoon of liquid (soy milk, milk, water, juice) to replace every egg or tablespoon of oil. (See page 202 for more about flaxseed.)

—Jan Shimp

LEMON VERBENA BREAD

½ cup unsalted butter
¼ cup fresh lemon verbena leaves, chopped
1 cup sugar
2 large eggs
Pinch of salt
½ cup milk
1½ cups sifted flour

1 tsp. baking powder
Grated rind of one lemon
¼ cup chopped nuts (optional)

Glaze: Mix together ½ cup sugar and 2 Tbsp. fresh lemon verbena leaves, finely chopped, with the juice of one lemon

For the bread, cream butter with verbena leaves in a mixer or food processor. Add sugar, eggs and milk and beat well. Add remaining ingredients, and pulse a few times until blended. Grease loaf pans (1 large, 2 small or 4 mini), and pour in batter. Bake at 350° F for 30–45 minutes, depending on pan size, or until toothpick inserted in center of bread comes out clean. Leave loaf in pan and pour glaze over loaf while still hot. Let sit several hours. Remove loaf from pan. Wrap in foil to ripen overnight if you like, or serve when cool. You can also freeze this bread for later use.

—Julie Manchester, Woodsong Herbals

BUTTERMILK AND HERB ICE CREAM

This frozen treat is a hit in the summertime and tastes like frozen yogurt.

2 quarts buttermilk
1 quart whipping cream
2 cups sugar
1½ tsp. vanilla
2 tsp. each fresh lemon balm and lemon verbena

Combine all ingredients and pour into a 1-gallon ice cream freezer. Follow freezer directions. Makes 3 quarts.

—Penny King

COCONUT MILK ICE

Coconuts are very healthful. They are a natural (unsprayed) food on sale in most countries. The milk is not pasteurized, and the flesh can be enjoyed and digested raw, fresh from the nut.

3 egg whites
3 cups powdered sugar
Juice of one medium lemon
3 cups fresh coconut milk

1½ cups coconut flesh, finely grated
grated vanilla stick for garnish

Whip the egg whites until stiff, then blend in the sugar and lemon juice. Add the coconut milk and flesh, mix very well and whip all together until stiff. Put into ice cube trays and freeze. Before eating, sprinkle with grated vanilla stick. Delicious!

—Juliette de Bairacli Levy, reprinted with permission from *Nature's Children*

BREAKFAST DISHES

NETTLES FLORENTINE

4 cups washed chopped nettles
3 Tbsp. low-fat cream cheese
4 organic eggs
Salt, pepper

In a frying pan at medium heat, stir in the nettles and low-fat cream cheese. Cook for about 3 minutes. Make 4 little nests in the nettles and add an egg to each of the indentations. Cover and cook until the eggs are done. Serve atop a slice of whole grain toast. Top it off with some salsa if you like. Serves 4.

—Brigitte Mars

Basil

Basil has been called the king of all herbs. It certainly is the most pop-ular and familiar kitchen herb. There is a lot of folklore surrounding this herb. In India the basil plant is sacred to both Krishna and Vishnu. Considered to be an aphrodisiac, an appetite enhancer and a spirit-lifter, basil is primarily an edible herb. Cooks all over the world highly value basil for its pungent, spicy flavor. As a medicinal tea, it has been used to relieve fevers, colds and headaches.

SWEET BASIL TOFU OMELETTE

1 tsp. butter
¾ cup tofu
1 egg
1 clove garlic

1 Tbsp. chopped chives or onion
1 Tbsp. fresh chopped basil (or 1 tsp. dried)
⅓ cup Cheddar cheese

Melt butter in skillet. Mash tofu and beat together with 1 egg. Add garlic, chives and basil. Pour mixture into skillet and cook until firm. Turn heat off, drop cheese on top, cover pan and allow a couple minutes to melt. Serves 2.

—RISA MORNIS

MAKE-AHEAD SAUSAGE AND DANDELION BREAKFAST

2½ cups seasoned croutons
1 lb. breakfast sausage
3 cups fresh dandelion leaves, chopped
4 eggs
2¼ cups milk
1 10½-oz. can cream of mushroom soup
1 4-oz. jar pimentos, drained
1 cup each sharp cheddar and Monterey jack cheese, shredded
¼ tsp. dry mustard
Herb sprigs and carrot curls (for garnish)

Spread croutons on bottom of greased 13- x 9-inch baking dish. Crumble sausage into large skillet. Cook over medium heat until browned, stirring occasionally. Bring heat to low; add dandelion leaves and sauté just until wilted. Drain any drippings. Spread dandelion and sausage over croutons. Set aside. Whisk eggs and milk in large bowl until blended. Stir in soup, pimentos, cheeses and mustard. Pour egg mixture over sausage, dandelion and croutons. Refrigerate overnight. When ready to bake, preheat oven to 325°F. Bake 50–55 minutes or until set and lightly browned on top. Garnish with herb sprigs and carrot strips or curls, if desired. Refrigerate leftovers. Serves 10–12.

—PETER GAIL, REPRINTED WITH PERMISSION FROM *THE GREAT DANDELION COOKBOOK*.

DANDELION PANCAKES

1 cup fresh dandelion petals
½ cup whole wheat pastry flour
½ cup unbleached white flour
1 tsp. baking powder
½ tsp. baking soda

1 Tbs. raw sugar
1 egg
1 cup milk or soy milk
1 tsp. vanilla

Collect a colander full of dandelion blossoms. Wash and remove their green caps. Set aside the petals. Combine the dry ingredients. Beat in the wet ingredients and stir the dandelion petals into the batter. Add a little more milk if a thinner pancake is desired. Heat a griddle with oil or butter and pour the batter on in big spoonfuls. Flip over when bubbles ring the edges of the cakes. Serve with maple syrup. Makes 8–12 small pancakes.

—RISA MORNIS

FRESH ELDERBERRY SYRUP

This is heavenly on French toast. Be sure you use the blue/black elderberries, not the toxic red ones.

8 cups fresh elderberries
4½ cups apple juice
2½ tsp. agar powder, (optional)
2 cups honey
Juice of one lemon or ¼ tsp. of ascorbic acid powder

Add the elderberries to 4 cups of the apple juice (reserve ½ cup) and bring to a boil. Simmer 10 minutes, covered. Meanwhile, soak the agar powder in a little water to soften. Mash the berries well in the pot and strain out seed and pulp. A Foley food mill works well. Add the reserved apple juice to the pulp, mix well and strain again. You should have about 7 cups of strained elderberry juice. Add honey and agar, bring to a boil and boil for 2 minutes. (The agar thickens the syrup, but is optional.) Add lemon juice or ascorbic acid to retain color. You may bottle and freeze the syrup or process it for storage. This recipe works well for rose hip syrup, also. However, it requires several strainings to remove all the fuzz. Makes 2 quarts.

—Mindy Green

FLAX PANCAKES

To your favorite pancake mix for 4 or 5 servings, add ½ cup freshly ground flaxseed (use a seed grinder or a blender). Cook as usual. You don't notice the flaxseed at all except for an improvement in texture.

—Cathy Gileadi-Sweet

Flax

There are two kinds of essential fatty acids (EFAs) that are essential to good health: omega–6s and omega–3s. More than 80 percent of the U.S. population is severely deficient in omega-3 fats. This results in a multitude of health problems including obesity, nervous system conditions, immune system failures, behavior problems, depression, digestive difficulties and every kind of skin disease. Most fish contains some omega-3s, but not everyone eats fish regularly. Dried beans, purslane and spinach are other good sources. But, perhaps the most reliable way to get your omega–3s is through flax. After a good deal of experimentation, I have come to prefer flaxseeds themselves to the more expensive, highly perishable flaxseed oil. If you can get absolutely fresh, organic flaxseed oil, you can use it to make smoothies or to put on your salad. Flaxseeds are cheap, mild-tasting and easy to use. Try these recipes for a few days, and you'll be amazed at how soft your skin feels, how calm you're feeling, how well your bowels are working and how alert and strong you seem to be. If you're overweight, you're going to be surprised: adequate EFAs will help you lose weight.

—Cathi Gileadi-Sweet

FLAX FOR CEREAL

To your bowl of hot cereal add some freshly ground flaxseeds and brown sugar. Top with soy milk. A very substantial and filling breakfast.

—Cathy Gileadi-Sweet

THE DAILY FLAX SHAKE

3 Tbsp. flaxseed
1 cup soy milk or other milk
2–3 Tbsp. jam (or other sweetener)

Place flaxseed in blender container and blend. Add other ingredients and blend until smooth. Add more soy milk if a thinner shake is wanted. Drink immediately. This is thick and has a definite texture, but it's mild and tasty. Drink in the morning, and you won't want anything else for breakfast.

—Cathy Gileadi-Sweet

DANDELION BREAKFAST SMOOTHIE

Take a large handful of fresh dandelion leaves, 1 apple, 1 Tbsp. apple cider vinegar and maybe 1 or 2 carrots. Blend in a VitaMix blender and take as a morning vitamin pill/breakfast drink. The benefit? It is loaded with more vitamins and minerals, including all the trace minerals, than you can count. Greg Tilford, prominent herbalist and writer, claims dandelion is one of the most complete foods man can eat, and I concur with him.

—Peter Gail, reprinted with permission from
The Great Dandelion Cookbook.

APPENDIX OF HEALING HERBS

The following herb chart is useful as a quick reference to the medicinal qualities of each herb. One herb can be used in different ways for many problems. The key to the chart will tell the most common way of using the herb. (Tea, extract, eating, essential oil, etc.) If an herb is used in more than one way, two key letters divided by a slash will appear. Look in the index under each herb for the recipes which include them.

Key

T = Tea or extract.

E = Eat in salads, dips, sandwiches, soups, etc. (Look in index for recipes with this herb).

Cp = Capsule or pill.

G = Gargle with tea made of this herb.

S = Syrup made of water, herb and sweetener.

Es = Essential oil diluted and applied externally.

O = Natural oil of the seed, taken internally.

Ex = External application either as a poultice, compress or liniment. A compress is a cloth soaked in hot herbal tea and applied to skin until cool. A liniment is a combination of herbs infused in rubbing alcohol or oil and applied externally. See below for poultice description.

B = Used in a bath (including foot or hand baths). Make a big pot of herbal tea and pour into bath, or put herb in a cloth bag and steep in the bath water.

P = Poultice the herb by bruising the fresh herbs or making a paste of water and dry herbs. Apply to a piece of cloth, cover with gauze, and apply to skin. Remove it when it starts to feel uncomfortable. The same poultice can be reused a number of times.

	Allergies, asthma	Anxiety, nervous system	Arthritis, rheumatism	Colds, flu, fever	Constipation	Diarrhea	Digestive tonic	Headache	Heart problems	Indigestion	Infection	Liver/blood problems	Lung problems	Menstrual problems	Nutritional	Skin problems	Sore throat	Urinary problems
Alfalfa			E		E		E					E			E	E		T
Amaranth						T								T	E	T/E	G	T/E
Angelica			T	T/S			T			T			T	T				T
Astragalus	T			T			T/E				T	T	T					
Basil		T		T	T/E		E	T		T/E	T				E			T/E
Black haw		T				T				T			T	T				
Black pepper			E	E						E							S	
Borage		T		T						T					O	E		
Burdock root			T/E		E		T/E			T/E	T	T/E				T/E		T
Calendula	T/E									T/E	T			T				
Cardamom								T		T/E								
Catnip		T		T						T	T	T						
Cayenne	E/Cp	Cp/Ex	Cp/E				E			E/Cp	E/Cp	Cp	E					
Celery seed		T	T				E			T				T				
Chamomile		T	T				T	T		T	T			T				
Chickweed			T/E		E/T		E				T				E			
Chicory					T		E			T					E			
Cinnamon					Cp/E					Cp/E	Cp/E	T						
Coriander			Ex	T	T/E	T/E	E			T/E	T							
Cronewort (mugwort)		T		T											T	E		
Cumin										Cp/E	Cp/E			Cp/E	E			
Damiana		T					T											
Dandelion			T/E		E		E/T					T/E			T/E	E	T/E	

	Allergies, asthma	Anxiety, nervous system	Arthritis, rheumatism	Colds, flu, fever	Constipation	Diarrhea	Digestive tonic	Headache	Heart problems	Indigestion	Infection	Liver/blood problems	Lung problems	Menstrual problems	Nutritional	Skin problems	Sore throat	Urinary problems
Dill										T/E					E			
Echinacea	T		T								T	T	T				T	T
Elderflower			T								T		T				G	
Elderberry			T/E	T/S							T						S	
Fennel leaf/seed				T/S			E			T/E	T				E			
Fenugreek seed					T/E	E/T				T/E			T				G	
Flaxseed			Ex		T/E		E						T	O	E			T
Garlic	Cp/E		Cp/E	Cp/E			E		Cp/E	Cp/E	Cp/E	E	Cp/E		E			
Ginger root		T	Ex	T			E	T	T	T/Cp	T	T		T/E			S/E	
Ginseng root		T	T				T		T		T			T				
Hops flower/pollen		T						T	T									
Horseradish	E		Ex				E			E	T	E						E
Lamb's quarters						T	E			E					E	T/E		
Lavender flower		Es/B	Ex/Es					T/Ex		T	T							
Lemon balm leaf		T	T	T					T	T/E	T							
Licorice root							T			T			T	T				
Lovage stem/leaf			T				E			T/E				E				
Mallow leaf/root	T			T/S			T/E				T		T/E	S	E		G	
Marjoram	T		E	S				T		T/E	T			T				
Meadowsweet			T	T		T		T		T	T							T
Mint		T	T			T	T/E	T		T	T							
Milk thistle				E/Cp		E/Cp	E/Cp			E/Cp			E/Cp					

	Allergies, asthma	Anxiety, nervous system	Arthritis, rheumatism	Colds, flu, fever	Constipation	Diarrhea	Digestive tonic	Headache	Heart problems	Indigestion	Infection	Liver/blood problems	Lung problems	Menstrual problems	Nutritional	Skin problems	Sore throat	Urinary problems
Mullein	T	T		T/S		T					T		S				G	
Mustard			Ex	B/P	E		E						P					
Nettles	T/E		T	T			E					T/E		T		T/E		T
Oregano		T/E		T/E				T		T/E	T							
Parsley	T		T/E				E					T/E			E	T		T
Queen Anne's Lace (Wild Carrot)			T		T	T				T/E		T		T/E		T/E		
Red clover		E	T		T		E/T				T	T/E			E	T/E		
Red raspberry leaf		T		T	T	T					T			T	T			T
Rose		T						T	T							T	S	
Rose hip				T/S	T/E		E				T/Cp				E			T
Rosemary		T					E/T		T/E	T/E	T	T/E		T				
Sage		T		T/S		T	E	T		T/S	T	T/E	S				G	T/E
Skullcap		T						T				T		T				
Sweet cecily				T			E			E								
Tarragon		T					T											
Thyme				T/Es			E	T		T/E	T		T/Es				Es	G
Turmeric							E					T		T/E	E			
Violet	S		S		S		E	T			T		T		E	T/Es	G	
Vitex														T				
Watercress		E	E				E		E			E			E	E		E
Wild cherry bark	T/S			T/S			T						T/S					
Wild ginger							T/E								E			

	Allergies, asthma	Anxiety, nervous system	Arthritis, rheumatism	Colds, flu, fever	Constipation	Diarrhea	Digestive tonic	Headache	Heart problems	Indigestion	Infection	Liver/blood problems	Lung problems	Menstrual problems	Nutritional	Skin problems	Sore throat	Urinary problems
Wild yam		T	T							T				T				
Willow bark		T	T	T				T										
Wood betony		T					T						T					
Yarrow			T	T		T	T	T		T	T					T/Ex		T
Yellow dock			T		T		T/E					T/E	T		E	T		T

HERBALISTS' PROFILES

Jo-Ann Albano
Ladybug Knoll
Ocean Drive, Frenchboro
Long Island, ME 04635
Phone: 207-334-2979

Ladybug Knoll overlooks the ocean, providing inspiration for the many products created there. Every product is the result of Jo-Ann's love of gardens and herbs. Some of Ladybug Knoll's products are Boo Boo Cream (a highly concentrated cream made from organically grown healing herbs for cuts, bruises, sprains, problem dry skin and lip balm); Arthritis Balm (soothes hands, feet and joints and stimulates circulation); Lavender Hair Rinse; Pottery (whimsical birdhouses, garden signs, ornaments, tiles and bowls), and watercolors of herbs, garden scenes and whimsies. Jo-Ann also offers herb lectures on medicinal uses, companion planting, bee and butterfly gardens, beauty gardens and kitchen gardens (inside and out).

Susan Wittig Albert
Thyme & Seasons Books
P.O. Drawer M
Bertram, TX 78605

Susan Wittig Albert is the author of the *China Bayles Herbal Mysteries* and serves as editor and publisher of *China's Garden,* a newsletter celebrating the mysteries of herbs. She is a featured speaker at herb meetings and a member of the Herb Society of America, the International Herb Association and the Texas Herb Growers and Marketers Association. Her articles frequently appear in such publications as the *Herb Companion*.

Matthew Alfs
P.O. Box 11337
Minneapolis, MN 55411

Matthew Alfs is an herbal educator, free-lance writer and bookseller. Known to readers and students as "The Weedster," Matt teaches a three-part class on edible and medicinal wild plants every year. He writes for *Wild Foods Forum* and other national publications and is writing a book on edible and medicinal wild plants. He also puts out a quarterly catalog of books for sale (both new and out-of-print) on edible and medicinal wild plants and wilderness survival.

Sheryl Allyn
Wilderness Way
744 Glenmary Drive
Owego, New York 13827
Phone: 607-687-9186

Sheryl is a practicing herbalist and wildcrafter. At Wilderness Way Nature Awareness School, she teaches the blessings of the wild herbs used in medicine, food and survival. Sheryl continues to study nature skills and herbology with several mentors. Currently, she is reinforcing her personal medicine with doctorate work toward a Ph.D. in Naturopathy, expanding her expertise in homeopathic and nutritional healing therapies. Wilderness Way Primitive Skills/Tracking/Nature Awareness School, a 40-acre woodlot with pristine springs, 3-acre pond, overgrown fields, trails and organic gardens in upstate New York, was founded by Michael Head in 1994.

Sharleen Andrews-Miller

National College of Naturopathic Medicine
11231 Southeast Market Street
Portland, OR 97215
Phone: 503-255-7355

Sharleen Andrews-Miller is a faculty member at the National College of Naturopathic Medicine (NCNM) in Portland, Oregon. Shar teaches about the herbs of the Northwest, blending plant identification field trips, lectures and hands-on medicine making labs to both the medical students at NCNM as well as the general community.

Shar is also the assistant coordinator for the Portland Naturopathic Clinic's Medicinary (natural pharmacy) where she makes herbal medicines, fills prescriptions, orders herbs and supplements, educates students in medicine making and shares her enthusiasm for herbs. The Portland Naturopathic Clinic is the teaching clinic for NCNM, providing a learning experience for the medical students and an affordable source of naturopathic health care for the community.

Maia Ballis

Sun Mountain Center
35751 Oak Springs Drive
Tollhouse, CA 93667
Phone: 209-855-3710

Sun Mountain is a 40-acre land trust in the Sierra Nevada foothills between Yosemite and Sequoia National Parks with five acres of certified organic gardens and orchards and national forest on two sides. Much of the property is left wild for visitors to roam. Sun Mountain Center offers herb classes in which Maia shares her many years of herbal experience with small groups in intensive hands-on classes. The recipes shared here were reprinted from her *Sun Mountain Natural Foods Cookbook.* Sun Mountain also makes a number of herbal products and sells related items and books. There is an extensive library for member on-site use.

Robin Rose Bennett
25 Melrose Avenue
Upper Greenwood Lake, NJ 07421
Phone: 973-853-3463

Robin Rose Bennett completed an apprenticeship with Susun Weed in 1985 and has been teaching herbal medicine and earthspirit healing under the name WiseWoman Healing Ways since 1986. She has trained about 100 apprentices and taught thousands of students in the New York area and around the country. She has been a regularly featured guest on WBAI radio and television's "Alive and Wellness" show and has also been featured in many newspaper and magazine articles on herbal healing. She is currently working on her first book, *Healing Magic: Wisdom of the Moon, Women, and Plants,* and has a private consultation practice in New York City.

Peter Bigfoot
Reevis Mountain School of Self-Reliance
HCO 2, Box 1534
Roosevelt, Arizona 85545
Phone: 520-467-2675

Peter Bigfoot is an herbalist specializing in, but not limited to, southwestern U.S. herbology. He is a pioneer in the discovery of important uses of previously unknown southwestern plants. In 1979 Peter founded the Reevis Mountain School of Self-Reliance, which focuses on teaching outdoor living skills, native herbology, natural healing and organic gardening. The school offers a line of tinctures made from their home-grown and wildcrafted herbs.

Sage Blue
Wolf Howl Herbals
RR #1, Earthwings Farm
Orange, VT 05641
Phone: 802-479-1034

Wolf Howl Herbals derives from Sage Blue's passionate interest in the folk-loric herstory of women—the midwives, witches and herbalists who have been developing and using plant medicine since the beginning of time.

"Making a cup of herbal tea," says Sage, "is a deep ritual for me. I feel countless wise women preparing cups of tea to ease childbirth, ward off a cold, reduce a fever, warm a chill, calm a troubled heart, cool a hot flash, strengthen bones. I feel gratitude for the magic of the plants waiting to be released by the alchemy of water, fire and prayer. The aroma wafts into my body, preparing me for the healing touch of the Mother's hand. Truth, beauty and natural order come together in a simple cup of tea."

In the spring, summer and fall, visitors are invited to visit the herb garden, labyrinth, wildcrafting fields and woods and to attend ongoing classes called "Sacred Earth, Sacred Medicine."

Mary Bove, N.D.
Brattleboro Naturopathic Clinic
1063 Marlboro Road
Brattleboro, VT 05301

Dr. Mary Louise Bove obtained her Doctorate of Naturopathic Medicine and Midwifery Certification from Bastyr College of Natural Health Sciences in Seattle, WA. She also received a Diploma of Phytotherapy/Herbal Medicine at the School of Phytotherapy in Great Britain and is a member of the National Institute of Medical Herbalists, London. She served as a full-time faculty member at Bastyr College, in the departments of Botanical Medicine and Naturopathic Midwifery and was Chair of the Botanical Medicine Department from 1990–1993. Currently, she practices naturo-pathic family medicine, including natural childbirth, at the Brattleboro Naturopathic Clinic, in Brattleboro, Vermont. She lectures throughout North America in the fields of botanical medicine, phytotherapy and naturopathic obstetrics.

Carole Brown
3235 South Barcelona Street
Spring Valley, CA 91977-3005
Phone: 619-466-5009
email: cbrown@millennianet.com

Carole Brown is a practicing clinical herbalist who trained under Amanda McQuade Crawford at Self Heal School. She teaches classes on medicinal herbs as well as metaphysical classes related to herbs. She lives with her husband, two cats and a dog and grows many medicinal herbs, culinary herbs and native plants that are used medicinally.

Jane Carden
10 Kipling Avenue
Epsom, Auckland 1003, New Zealand 09-630-3076

Jane Carden has been president of the Auckland Herb Society for the last two years. Her interest in herbs began 24 years ago when few kitchens had more than a packet of mixed dried herbs, and anyone keen on herbs was considered a crank. Jane has a Cordon Bleu certificate but doesn't consider herself a "professional" cook, only a good basic cook. She has owned her own café and catered from home. Currently, Jane writes a cooking column for an herb magazine and gives demonstrations to small groups.

Pat Chichon
31 North Hill Road
Ringoes, NJ 08551
Phone: 609-466-3945
Email: Pakajomi@aol.com

Pat Chichon is a farmer, herbalist, nutritional consultant and nurse practitioner. Most of the food she and her family eat, the fuel they use and the herbs they use nutritionally and medicinally come from their land and their community, which Pat has served since the 70s. She has also taught throughout New Jersey, in Pennsylvania and New York. Pat is currently working with people who have chronic and acute health and disease issues. She continues teaching and sharing her recipes and knowledge of the power and gentleness of the herbal healing arts.

Russ Cohen
90 Everett Street
Arlington, MA 02174

Russ Cohen is a professional environmentalist and wild foods enthusiast. He has been employed by the Riverways Program of the Massachusetts Department of Fisheries, Wildlife and Environmental Law Enforcement since 1988 and has served as its Rivers Advocate since 1992. Russ is in his 22nd year of teaching courses about wild edibles. Last year he taught over 30 courses for over a dozen different organizations including the New England Wild Flower Society, the Boston Museum of Science and the Appalachian Mountain Club. Russ and his wife Ellen Vliet host an annual Harvest Party for their friends for which they prepare several dozen dishes (appetizers, soups, salads, main courses, desserts, condiments, and hot and cold beverages) from wild ingredients.

Althea Dixon
Professional Scribe
3310 West Bell Road, #221
Phoenix, Arizona 85023

The author of *Aunt Althea's Homespun Homilies*, Althea Dixon is enthusiastic about cooking foods that not only look good, taste good and smell good, but also are highly nutritious. Since it is difficult to find nonhybrid vegetables today, Althea puts her emphasis on weeds, which she considers about the only plants left which have maintained their genetic diversity and vigor. Althea studied with "Weed Woman" Linda Runyon.

Ruth Dreier
11 Howells Road
Belmont, MA 02178
Phone: 617-422-1921

Ruth Dreier is a practicing herbalist, aromatherapist and flower essence practitioner in the Cambridge, Massachusetts area. She holds a B.A. in Botanical Sciences, is both nationally and internationally certified in aromatherapy, has apprenticed with herbalist and wildcrafter Dr. Ryan Drum, holds a Master Herbalist certificate and is the staff herbalist for Harnett's, an herbal store in Cambridge. She teaches courses at the Boston Center for Adult Education, Brookline Community Education, Interface, Bread and Circus, Cambridge Natural Foods and for private companies in the Boston, Cape Cod and Martha's Vineyard areas, and currently offers apprenticeship courses in both herbal medicine and flower essences. In private consultations, Ruth utilizes herbs, aromatherapy and flower essences to create a complete and nourishing herbal approach to physical disease and emotional and spiritual well-being.

Donna d'Terra
P.O. Box 382
Willits, CA 95490
Phone: 707-459-5030

 Donna d'Terra has been growing and gathering plants for food and medicine for the past decade on the land where she lives, in the hills of Mendocino County in northern California. She is a graduate of the California School of Herbal Studies and now teaches an herbal apprentice course for women that includes herbal therapeutics, medicine making, flower essences, herb gardening, aromatherapy, cooking with herbs, wild gathering and ethnobotany. Donna also has a small herbal medicine business, Down-to-Earth Herbs. She also earns her livelihood as a craftswoman and storyteller.

Kathleen Duffy
Herbarium
264 Exchange Street
Chicopee, MA 01013
Phone: 413-598-8119

Kathleen Duffy is a nurse and herbalist, and the owner of the Herbarium in Chicopee, Mass. Kathleen earned her Master Herbalist certification at Dominion Herbal College in Vancouver, BC, studied at the Shook Institute of Herbal Pharmacology as well as with renowned teachers such as Linus Pauling, Ph.D., John Christopher, N.D., Harold Manner, Ph.D., Albert Szent-Gyorgyi, Ph.D., Christopher Hobbs, David Hoffmann, Joseph Issels, N.D. and Douglas Elliot, M.H. Kathleen has taught classes on herbal medicine for almost 20 years and has been a guest on many TV and radio programs. Currently, she is the host of the weekly one-hour radio show, "Herbs for Health and Healing," which can be heard on WNNZ AM 540, broadcasted in five states.

Judy Dunning and Bonnie Pastor
Southwest Herbs
15255 Lyons Valley Road
Jamul, CA 91935
Phone: 619-669-0222
Email: npastor@mail.sdsu.edu

Sisters Judy Dunning and Bonnie Pastor operate the Wild Sage Herb Ranch in Jamul, California and publish a newsletter called *Southwest Herbs*. The newsletter is packed with information about the many ways to use herbs such as starting an herb garden, making medicinal herbal preparations and craft uses. Everything has a Southwest focus, from the kind of recipes included to the in-depth "Herb of the Month" article. A column called "Everyday Herbs" tells how to grow and use the basic culinary herbs, and there is a question-and-answer column for the herb gardener struggling with the Southwest climate, plus much more.

Judy is a life-long student of horticulture. As part of her experience as a canyoneer for the San Diego Natural History Museum and as a member of the California Native Plant Society, she has become knowledgeable in native herb plants of the Southwest. Bonnie is an herbalist, life-long gardener, cook, researcher and writer. Together they are the co-founders of the Herb Club of San Diego. They also give programs and teach classes about herbs in San Diego.

Jane Dwinell
R.D. 1, Box 37A
Irasburg, VT 05845
Email: sky@together.net

Jane Dwinell is a nurse healer with a private practice in Healing Touch and Spiritual Direction, an author (*Birth Stories: Mystery, Power, and Creation*), maple syrup producer and Unitarian Universalist minister serving a small parish in Derby Line, Vermont. She has an extensive cultivated herb garden and forages for wild plants to supply her family with all their culinary and medicinal herb needs. Jane lives in northern Vermont with her partner and two children on their 45-acre solar-powered homestead.

Tina Finneyfrock
Mountain Spring Herbals
R.D. 1, Box 43Y
Earlville, NY 13332
Email: TinFin@juno.com

Tina Finneyfrock has studied herbs and healing traditions for 19 years. She is a certified childbirth educator, a Master Herbalist and holistic therapist who earned her degrees from Wild Rose College of Natural Healing in Canada. She holds certificates in Homeopathy, Iridology and Women's Health. Originally from the Washington, D.C. area, Tina has established six herb and flower gardens during her 15 years at Mountain Spring Homestead. She also tends a quarter-acre organic vegetable garden which provides the family with a bounty of natural foods. In addition to teaching workshops, Tina maintains a holistic health consulting practice, lectures on herbs and related topics and has published *Wholisic Healing for the Family*.

Her life's work is to pass on the knowledge of the natural world taught to her by her grandparents.

Dr. Peter A. Gail

Goosefoot Acres Press
P.O. Box 18016
Cleveland, OH 44116-0016
216-932-2145

Peter Gail founded and directs the Goosefoot Acres Center for Wild Vegetable Research and Education in Cleveland, Ohio. He is the author of several books on using backyard weeds as food and writes a regular column, "On the Trail of the Volunteer Vegetable," in *The Business of Herbs,* an international trade journal for herb growers and marketers. Gail's articles on wild foods have also appeared in regional and national magazines.

Peter began eating wild foods as a young boy after his father's untimely death. A family friend showed Peter's mother that they could eat well off the wild vegetables growing in their ten-acre backyard until she was able to support the young family. Gail holds a Ph.D. in botany from Rutgers University and was a professor of Urban and Environmental Studies at Cleveland State University for 16 years. He has spent the last 25 years researching how various ethnic groups use weeds for food. In 1988, Gail left the university to found the Goosefoot Acres Center, through which he continues his research and shares his work. In addition to *The Dandelion Celebration, A Guide to Unexpected Cuisine,* Gail has also authored the *Goosefoot Acres Volunteer Vegetable Sampler* (soon to be published in a newly titled second edition), *The Totally Free Lunch: A Consumer's Guide to Volunteer Vegetables* and *The Delightful Delicious Daylily,* as well as collections of recipes for purslane, lamb's quarters and violets.

Colette Gardiner
P.O. Box 10914
Eugene, OR 97440
Email: coletteg@efn.org

Colette Gardiner is an herbal teacher and obsessive gardener. She is a co-founder and teacher of the Women's Herbalist Conference, now in its ninth year. She is coowner of Blue Iris Botanicals, writes for the We'moon Almanac and offers an eight-month herbal studies program. She also offers herb walks and classes on all aspects of herbalism. Colette has been working with plants for 18 years and is magically assisted by her two cats.

Cascade Anderson Geller
1934 Southeast 56th Avenue
Portland, OR 97215
Phone: 503-232-0473

Wise woman wildcrafter, lover/teacher of all things herbal, mother and daughter of the earth—American herbalism has been a part of Cascade Anderson Geller's life since she was a small girl. Her heritage includes herbs and midwifery practiced by her great grandmothers. Her training came from them as well as from Dominion Herbal College and years of personal study in the forest, field and kitchen. Cascade spent 13 years as the botanical instructor at the National College of Naturopathic Medicine in Oregon, and has had a variety of private and joint practices with naturopathic physicians, chiropractors and medical doctors.

Cathy Gileadi-Sweet
Cathy Gileadi, Editing, Etc.
110 West Aspen Way
Salem, UT 84653
Phone: 801-423-9125
Email: cgileadi@itsnet.com

Cathy Gileadi-Sweet is a free-lance writer and editor specializing in herbal medicine. About 18 years ago, she started working with Dr. John R. Christopher, the famous herbalist, editing his work and writing for him. Over the years she has had a hand in almost all of the Christopher publications. She wrote *Everywoman's Herbal,* a compilation of Dr. Christopher's stories about treating women herbally (compiled posthumously) and her own research and life stories. In addition, Cathy works with the Nebo Institute of Herbology, a local group that promotes current research and publishing on herbal medicine.

The mother of nine children, Cathy tends a medicinal herb garden and also likes to gather herbs in the wild. She has also studied homeopathy, iridology and other modalities.

In addition to her herbal interests, Cathy is a belly dancer who performs with a traditional folkloric troupe in local venues. She also writes poetry, which occasionally appears in literary journals.

Judith Graves
Lambs & Thyme
240 Bullock Road
Richmond, NH 03470
Phone: 603-239-8621

Judith Graves started Lambs & Thyme in 1991 when she retired from teaching. Soon herb gardens began to grow and needed to be shared, so Lambs & Thyme opened its doors to the public. Today, a much-expanded Lambs & Thyme offers garden teas and tours, lectures and several workshops throughout the year. Three retired sheep—Sweet Annie, Pennyroyal and Sage—roam the property and enjoy visitors. They also share their wool with several projects. Lambs & Thyme focuses on culinary mixes, dips, medicinals, teas and herbal crafts. Over 120 natural products are available. The company also offers Cooking with Herbs classes, wreath classes and more.

Mindy Green
4133 Amber Street
Boulder, CO 80304-0957
Phone: 303-447-9552

Mindy Green has a background in herbalism spanning 24 years. Her fascination with the healing power of plants led to the study of aromatherapy in 1978. With over a decade of experience in the natural foods industry in the U.S. and Canada, she is also a licensed esthetician and massage practitioner and holds a degree in Wholistic Health Sciences. An herbalist, aromatherapist and cosmetics consultant, Mindy is a faculty member of the California School of Herbal Studies and the Rocky Mountain Center for Botanical Studies where she draws on 15 years of teaching experience to share her skills in herbal and cosmetic preparations, laboratory procedure, aromatherapy, plant identification, natural skin care and wild foods cooking. She is cofounder and consultant for Simplers Botanical Co., a founding member of the American Herbalists Guild and associate editor of the *American Herb Association Newsletter.* She has lectured in the U.S. and Canada and is a contributing writer to several aromatherapy and herb publications. Mindy is proud to contribute to the herbal renaissance in America and has coauthored a book on the use of essential oils and herbs called *Aromatherapy, A Complete Guide to the Healing Art.* She is also author of the Keats Good Herb Guide, *Calendula.* Mindy currently works at the Herb Research Foundation and teaches aromatherapy and herb classes in Boulder, Colorado.

Melissa J. Hertzler
Honeybee Gardens
141 Heather Lane
Wyomissing, PA 19610
Phone: 610-478-9090

Melissa Hertzler started Honeybee Gardens in 1995. She had studied herbs casually for years and decided to put that knowledge to use in order to save her husband's face (his skin was hypersensitive to commercial shaving products). It took time. Her husband sampled formulas on almost a daily basis. One was too gentle. Another wasn't soothing. With each trial, the results were documented. More research ensued. Finally, one day, he proclaimed, "This is it!" and Herbal Aftershave was born. By now, Melissa was also creating moisturizers, powders and other preparations in addition to the aftershave, while making her living in the corporate world. But corporate life for Melissa left much to be desired. After working eight hours a day in sterile, sickly environments, Melissa retreated to her gardens for solace and then to her herbal library to learn more about herbs. She became seduced by glorious useful plants. Soon afterwards, Honeybee Gardens was born.

Says Melissa: "I really feel that men have been overlooked when it comes to body care products. Our desire is to create beneficial body care products from only the finest and purest ingredients and offer these items to women and men. We make stuff that *really works* and we make it from ingredients you have heard of and can pronounce. We grow many of the herbs that go into our preparations—our way of making sure that only the best chemical-free botanicals are used. We are environmentally and humanely aware and try to provide some humor and happiness to others through our written words and products. We honestly believe in our body care products, and hope their benefits can be experienced by all."

Caroline Holmes
Denham End Farm, Denham
Bury St. Edmunds
Suffolk, 1P29 5EE, England
Phone/Fax: 01284-810653

Caroline Holmes is a well-known British herbalist and horticulturist. She has studied at the East Suffolk College of Agriculture and Horticulture and has received the Royal Horticultural Society's Gardener's Certificate. From 1979 to 1993 she ran an herb nursery, starting with wholesale contract propagation of herbs and trees and evolving into Caroline Holmes Herbs. She creates award-winning displays at international shows, offers simple courses on site and gourmet courses elsewhere. Caroline's courses combine her practical horticultural and culinary skills with her in-depth knowledge of plant history and food. She broadcasts on television and radio, has published a booklet on herbal teas and drinks and is chairman of the Herb Society.

Ellen Evert Hopman
P.O. Box 219
Amherst, MA 01004

Ellen Evert Hopman is an herbalist, counselor and author, living and working in an oak forest in western Massachusetts. She is the vice president of the international Druid order, The Henge of Keltria, and a human companion to two cats, Cerridwen and Myrddin. In addition to teaching classes and workshops on herbalism and nature spirituality in the United States and Europe, she has authored the following books: *Tree Medicine, Tree Magic,* a book on the herbal and magical properties of some common North American trees; *A Druid's Herbal For The Sacred Earth Year,* which describes the eight major religious festivals of the ancient Druids with suggestions for using herbs to celebrate them and other events such as weddings, funerals, baby blessings and house blessings; and *People of The Earth—The New Pagans Speak Out,* a book of interviews with pagan leaders from the United States and Canada. Ellen has also authored numerous videos and audiotapes, among them a video on identifying herbs and preparing basic herbal remedies.

Jo Jenner
P.O. Box 14654
Portland, OR 97214
Phone: 503-234-0142

Jo Jenner is a scientist by nature and a naturopathic physician by training. Her motto, "Health begins at home," expresses her deep-seated joy in helping find the healing equations in our own homes and backyards. "Herbs are your food and medicine, use them. Create new ways to increase your daily herbal intake." Dr. Jo communicates practical information in an entertaining and humorous manner. She is known for her dynamic delivery and timely relevant ideas, her mixture of knowledge, humor, practicality and enthusiasm.

Feather Jones
Rocky Mountain Center for Botanical Studies
P.O. Box 19254
Boulder, CO 80308-2254
Phone: 303-442-6861
Fax: 303-442-6294

The Rocky Mountain Center for Botanical Studies was founded in September of 1992 by herbalist Feather Jones, who recognized the growing need and demand to spread the knowledge of plants as medicines. RMCBS offers a 10-month residential training program exploring many aspects of western herbalism. While the curriculum is based on a solid foundation of plant and human sciences, a large portion of time is also spent in the field learning directly from the plants.

In 1995, the school added a second year advanced internship program in Clinical Herbalism, which is designed to enhance its students' professional skills and increase their herbal knowledge.

RMCBS places strong emphasis on the philosophy of bioregionalism. A large portion of the plants emphasized in the curriculum are those plants, native and naturalized, that are indigenous to the western United States. By educating people about using local plants, RMCBS contributes to helping protect the more popular and overharvested plants, such as echinacea and goldenseal.

Michael Jonas Kahn
Nutritional Science
ZKahn pH Balance Program
3619 East First Street, Suite 5
Long Beach, California 90803
Internet: http:/www.zphbalance.com
Email: drz@zphbalance.com

Michael Jonas Khan is a holistic doctor with a Ph.D. in Nutritional Science from the American College of Life Science, Austin, Texas, with 30 years experience in the study, teaching and practice of natural healing techniques.

He is currently the creator of the pH balance theory, a revolutionary self-evaluative body chemistry analysis health and diet education program which can be found on the Internet at www.zphbalance.com. It has helped many people over the years take an objective look at their health and provides them with a simple nutritional approach to bring themselves back into balance.

Bryan Ray Keith
1474 East McDaniel
Springfield, MO 65802

Bryan Ray is a simpler by nature, preferring to use common wild plants one or two at a time. He is also an artist, inventor, chef, psychic and herbalist. He has developed many delicious recipes for food and health and has unlimited innovative ideas and products now available to the general public by mail. His salad dressings are also available in dry form. Questions, medical problems and recipe requests can be addressed to him.

Penny King
300 Skyline Road
Georgetown, TX 78628

Penny King has been interested in herbs for many years. Presently she works for the American Botanical Council as coordinator of *HerbalGram,* the highly acclaimed scientifically-based journal on herbal medicine. Her other passion is to help coordinate ethnobotanical trips to Central and South America for pharmacists to study pharmacy from the rainforest in the world's greatest classroom—the rainforest itself. In addition to four trips with pharmacists to the rainforests, Penny has taught a workshop with 100 students and their families at the Amazon Center for Environmental Education and Research, studying medicinal plants. While managing a small herb business in Georgetown, Texas, for four years, Penny was on the founding board of directors of the Texas Herb Growers and Marketers Association. When not in the rainforests she can be found in Austin at the

American Botanical Council, brokering herbs, spices or oils through Bee Creek Botanicals or teaching classes through community schools on the many uses of herbs.

Henriette Kress
Pihlajatie 39 A 6 hc
Helsinki, Finland FIN-00270
Email: HeK@hetta.pp.fi

Henriette Kress is a commercial herb advisor in Finland who teaches commercial herb pickers how to harvest herbs that meet industry standards. Wildcrafting is her passion; she loves to walk in the woods, carefully harvesting greens, flowers, fruits, seeds, bark or roots as she goes. Unfortunately, not all of the really good herbs are available in Finland, so she keeps just a small herb plot—a low-maintenance garden where nettles and dandelions thrive. Henriette is also the keeper of one of the major herbal sites on the Internet: http://sunsite.unc.edu/herbmed. It's the home of the culinary and medicinal "herbfaqs" (FAQ means Frequently Asked Questions) as well as archives, pictures and other herbal lore.

Michelle and Tom Lawrenson
The Herbal Harvest
195R East Grove Street
Middleboro, MA 02346
Phone: 508-946-5005

Michelle and Tom Lawrenson run a small herb shop called Herbal Harvest which carries homemade herbal teas and dips and many aromatherapy blended herbal cosmetics. The mainstay of their business is herbal home parties, a perfect way to introduce people to the herbal lifestyle. They also do craft shows and fairs and teach herbal and aromatherapy classes.

Allie Letson
The Potted Herb
324 North Main Street
Amory, Mississippi 38821
Phone: 601-257-6032; 1-888-278-3474
Fax: 601-257-4035

Allie Letson is an herbalist/nurse working toward a Doctor of Naturopathy degree. She owns The Potted Herb, a wholesale, retail and mail-order company specializing in medicinal and culinary products. She offers her own gourmet herb and spice blends, coffee and teas; her aromatherapy products include custom-blended massage oils, bath oils, mineral bath salts, clay body masks and essential oils. She also sells medicinal and botanical salves, coffee, beeswax and herb candles, vitamins and potpourri. Allie publishes a newsletter called *The Herb & Spice Gazette,* does herb garden consulting, and holds workshops and lectures on a regular basis.

Juliette de Bairacli Levy
c/o Ash Tree Publishing
P.O. Box 64
Woodstock, NY 12498

Juliette de Bairacli Levy has spent more than half a century writing about her life in remote places and the lore she has learned as a friend and fellow traveler with tribes of gypsies. She has recently had two of her works expanded and reprinted by Ash Tree Publishing: *Common Herbs for Natural Health* and *Nature's Children,* from whence her recipes for this book come. *Nature's Children* is a classic of natural child rearing that deals not only with the physical complaints of pregnancy, birthing, nursing and raising children, but also with the needs of the spirit, soul and feelings of mother and child. Juliette is also the author of *The Complete Herbal Handbook for Farm and Stable, The Complete Herbal Handbook for the Dog and Cat, Traveler's Joy* and *Look! The Wild Swans.* She is known all over the world for her theories and techniques for the natural care of dogs, goats, horses and other animals.

Julie Manchester
Woodsong Herbals
P.O. Box 301
Randolph, VT 05060
Phone: 802-728-4941

Julie Manchester is the owner of Woodsong Herbals, a small herbal business dedicated to producing herbal products of exceptional quality. With her family, she maintains extensive organic gardens where she grows and ethically wildcrafts high quality herbs to use in vinegars, tinctures, salves, cosmetics and other herbal products. Her gardens are open to the public for walking and tasting, and she holds weed walks during the growing season. She also manages a retail space that offers herbal products, plants and other surprises from local artists.

Julie teaches herbal classes and workshops all over central and northern Vermont, as well as mentoring local high school students in herbal traditions. She considers herself a community herbalist. Says Julie, "I feel that educating the public is one of the best ways I can serve them."

Brigitte Mars
1919D 19th Street
Boulder, CO 80302-5508
Phone: 303-442-4967

Brigitte Mars, an herbalist and nutritional consultant, teaches herbology through the Rocky Mountain Center for Botanical Studies, Naropa Institute and the Boulder School of Massage Therapy. Brigitte has a weekly radio show and is the formulator for UniTea Herbs. Her tea blends, Mental ClariTea, SereniTea and SensualiTea are sold throughout the U.S. She often writes articles for *Let's Live,* and other publications and is the author of two books in the Keats Good Herb Guide series, *Elder* and *Herbs for Healthy Skin, Hair and Nails.*

Harvest McCampbell

7737 Fair Oaks Boulevard, #201
Carmichael, CA 95608
Phone: 916-558-0497

Harvest McCampbell is a naturalist and herbalist with over 20 years experience. She grew up eating and using wild plants under the care of her Native American grandmother and now shares this information and her encyclopedic knowledge of herbs through classes and her quarterly newsletter *Finding Your Way With Herbs.* Harvest harmoniously blends her Native American and Northern European heritage in her teachings. She offers seminars and training to beginning and advanced herb students. Her booklet *Sacred Smoke* has been a bestseller in new age and Native American shops on the West Coast for five years. She is currently working on two more booklets, *Working With Herbs* and *Cooking With Garlic.* In addition, she is a regular contributor to *Nature's Field,* a professional journal for practicing herbalists.

Christine McKenna

Herbal Earth
P.O. Box 56
Epsom, NH 03234
Phone: 603-226-1927
Fax: 603-463-7230

Christine McKenna's business, Herbal Earth, is a cottage industry of all-natural products and herbal supplies which are available at local stores, craft shows, herbal home parties and through mail order. This business grew from her love of herbs and plants. She says learning to acknowledge the many benefits plants offer us was a starting point. Then she began offering herbal gifts to family and friends. When the gifts were gone, requests for refills came in and the business sprouted.

Christine McKenna has studied with several New England herbalists and continues to add to and upgrade her skills. Many of the ingredients she uses in her creams and salves are gathered from the woods and fields in her own rural town. In addition to making products, Christine lectures and teaches classes both in her home and to various groups.

Christine also publishes an herbal newsletter with her friend and partner Michelle Parker. The *Herbal Earth Newsletter* is packed with in-depth herb reports, culinary recipes, craft ideas, sage advice, a calendar of herbal events, helpful tips and more.

Risa Mornis
Elda Mor Herbs
HCR 71, Box 4A
Reading, VT 05062
Phone: 802-484-9283

Natural medicine was a simmering interest for Risa Mornis at an early age. Her mother and grandmother both used homeopathic medicine, and her grandmother was also interested in herbs and reflexology. She went through school and college taking only arnica and other homeopathic medicines, avoiding aspirin and drugs. But her herbal education really began about 10 years ago as an employee of a Black Mountain, North Carolina health food store. Upon moving to Massachusetts she enrolled in a course on herbal therapeutics offered by Ellen Hopman. After a few years of more courses and self-study she started teaching basic herbal medicine courses, introducing people to herbs through plant identification walks and hands-on medicine making courses. Risa started a home-based herbal products company, making salves and tinctures with her own wildcrafted or organically grown herbs and selling them to local stores. Writing had always been an interest, so it was a natural next step to produce the *Village Herbalist* newsletter for Vermont and parts of New Hampshire, Massachusetts, New York and Maine. Risa eventually sold the newsletter and is now focusing on raising her children and writing. She continues to make and sell herbal products and teach classes. *An Herbal Feast* is her first book.

Sharon Murphy

Evergreen Herb Farm
24447 Highway 190
Lacombe, LA 70445
Phone: 504-674-0253

Sharon Murphy has been growing and using herbs to treat family needs since 1983 and has studied with such noted herbalists as Michael Tierra, David Hoffmann, Steven Foster, Selina Herron, Jim Duke and Ila Hernandez. She received her herbalist certificate from the Rosemary Gladstar one-year home study course. Sharon offers private herbal consultations, workshops and classes on a variety of topics including therapeutic herbalism, treating menopause naturally, herbs for stress, natural medicine for children, homeopathy and the Bach flower remedies, herbs for the immune system and more. She has spoken at the Wholistic Nurses Conference, the Biloxi Herb Fest and for garden shows and plant symposiums.

Andrea Murray

Plant Talk
38 Foreside Road
Cumberland, ME 04110
Phone: 207-781-3736

Since she became a vegetarian at age 16, Andrea has relied upon and incorporated plants into her daily life in many different ways. Cooking with vegetables, herbs and spices was the beginning, but her interest in plant nourishment soon spread to medicinal herbs and she began using various teas for her own health and well-being.

Andrea completed a nine-month intensive at the New Mexico Herb Institute, learning from Tieroana Klar Lowdog, then she headed back to Maine to continue studying medicinal herbs on her own. There, Andrea grows a wide variety of plants and has her own herbal product company, Plant Talk.

After studying with Janet Stetsor, she became a certified reflexologist, which she says beautifully complements herbalism. She co-owns the Foot Reflexology Center in Scarborough, Maine, where therapeutic sessions are offered along with herbal medicine consultations.

Suzanne Nagler
Wise Woman Herbal Guild
P.O. Box 102
Maple Falls, WA 98266-0102

An herbalist, wildcrafter and soapmaker, Suzanne and her husband care-take a 74-acre mountain, field and forest farm in northwest Washington near the Canadian border. Suzanne has studied with many wise women over the years including her 90+ year-old Aunt Mary who instilled in her a love for plants at a very early age. "I find my most inspiring teachers are the plants themselves. I build relationships with the plants by visiting them every day in their homes, sitting with them, getting to know them just as I would any person or animal." Suzanne is the owner of NettleSmith Cottage Gardens, a small, herbal apothecary on the farm offering high quality bulk herbs, organic tinctures, herbal soaps and salves, essential oils, candles, books, supplies and more. Suzanne teaches herbal workshops, study groups and apprenticeships. She specializes in teaching people to recognize and harvest wild plants, their medicinal and nutritional qualities and ethical wildcrafting.

Barbara Nardozzi
R.R. #2, Box 292
Hinesburg, VT 05461
Phone: 802-482-3500

Barbara is a certified and practicing herbalist with a degree in nutrition. From her home and gardens, she teaches about wild foods, cooking with edible flowers, creating a tea or medicine garden, and using herbs for health and well-being. As an herbalist, her focus is on long-term health support and chronic health problems. She loves wildcrafting and growing herbs for use in tinctures, teas and other preparations for family and friends. Her business, formerly called The Secret Garden, has been newly named Bram-blewood Herbs and Gardens.

Kathleen O'Mara
A Quality Herb Farm
P.O. Box 12937
Albuquerque, NM 87195
Fax: 505-452-8615
HerbNetMom@aol.com

Kathleen O'Mara learned about herbalism as a young woman when she was very ill. Conventional American medicine could do little for her, so she sought out alternative medicine and found the answer to her problems in her own backyard. After years of study and healing, she began to share her herbal knowledge through her business, A Quality Herb Farm and the Herb Network, a membership organization designed to facilitate the exchange of herbal information between herbalists of all ranges of experience.

Kathleen is currently continuing the historical study of herbalism, folk medicine and midwifery at the University of New Mexico.

Kiyra Page
1362 Islington Street
Portsmouth, NH 03801
Phone: 603-436-1402

Kiyra Page is an herbalist, gardener, writer, journalist, mother, grand-mother, channel and teacher. She planted her first flower, a lost, old-fashioned rosebush rescued from a weed patch beside the road, when she was seven years old. Fifty years later, she went to visit it—it was still growing. Now it is over seven feet high and covers a span of 20 feet or more, but it still blossoms, bearing delicate pink flowers with the tenacity of a mountain. She has come a long way from that seven-year-old with a vision, digging in the dirt and planting a twig, but the call from the Earth drew her back—this time to herbs.

Kiyra has studied all facets of herbology, beginning with cooking. As a natural progression, she began to see the more ancient use of herbs: for healing, health, and harmony. Kiyra studied independently, poring through modern texts and ancient herbal wisdom writings, and with teachers Deb Soule, Michael Teirra, Rosemary Gladstar, David Hoffmann and others.

Kirya is one of the cofounders of Page and Williams, Herbalists, a soap company. Currently she and her herbal partner, Mary Williams, make a line of 11 natural herbal soaps, soon to expand to other skin care, bath and home herbal products. Together they facilitate workshops throughout New England on skin care, soap making and the culinary and medicinal uses of herbs. She also conducts herb identification walks.

Mary Pat Palmer
52 Boylston Street, #1R
Boston, MA 02130
Phone: 617-524-5377
Email: Mpat@citysource.com
Web page: Http:/www.holistic.com/listings/02130mpl.html

Mary Pat Palmer, Boston's Urban Herbalist, is a licensed mental health counselor and herbal educator. Herbs are an integral part of her holistic psychotherapy practice, in which she works primarily with adult survivors of childhood sexual abuse, artists and those who are depressed. In addition to her private practice, Mary Pat researches alternative modes of treatment for her clients and gives talks and lectures about holistic psychotherapy and herbology and conducts weed walks and workshops on creating herbal products.

Herbal education began as a child for Mary Pat, with her mother and with her grandfather, a Cherokee Indian. She read Culpepper (a well-known 16th century herbalist) by kerosene lamp in the early 70s while organic farming at Earthworks, a back-to-the-land commune on the Canadian border in Vermont. In 1979 she went to Goddard College for graduate school in art therapy and then moved to Boston, where she established a community garden full of herbs and vegetables. She has been gardening ever since and guerrilla planting indigenous herbs in the parks of Boston.

Mary Pat believes that plant devas and plants contribute strongly to mental health and help us to connect with the universe, wherein lies our health. Her greatest happiness is often in providing safe alternatives to allopathic medications that have dangerous side effects.

Sonia Poitras
Earth Spirit Herbals
P.O. Box 223
White Bird, ID 83554

Sonia Poitras has been an herbalist for seven years. She lives in a remote part of Idaho where self-sufficiency and balance with the land are a way of life. She is the owner of Earth Spirit Herbals and teaches classes in herbalism for Earth Circle School of Wilderness Survival in Grangeville, Idaho. She also gives herbal consultations, makes personalized formulas and does spiritual healings.

Dr. H.S. Puri
Herba Indica
1160 D Vespian Way
Chesterfield, MO 63017
Phone: 914-684-2625
Email: Herbaindica@hotmail.com

Dr. H.S. Puri, a medical practitioner of Ayurveda, is a world-renowned pharmacognosist specializing in crude drugs used in traditional systems of Indian medicine. Dr. Puri worked for 16 years at the Pharmacognosy unit of Panjab University and then moved to the Central Institute of Medicinal and Aromatic Plants, a branch of the Indian Council of Medical Research. In 1986 he left the institute to start his own private consulting and manufacturing business. At present Dr. Puri supplies crude and finished botanical products all over the world. He also manufactures several health and beauty care products. Dr. Puri has over 50 research papers, articles and reviews to his credit. He is an honorary member of the National Institute of Medical Herbalists (UK) and a consultant to the American Herb Association.

Linda Quintana
Wonderland Tea & Spice
Alpine Herb Farm
6375 Rutsatz Road
Deming, WA 98244
Phone: 360-733-0517

For 20 years, Linda Quintana has been an herbalist, organic grower, wild-crafter and owner of Wonderland Tea & Spice and Alpine Herb Farm, a cottage industry located in the foothills of Mt. Baker where organic herbs are grown to be crafted into massage oils, teas, tinctures, vinegars and salves. Linda has dedicated her life to the study of herbs and to teaching people awareness of the importance of herbs on this planet and how they may enhance health. She regularly attends advanced seminars on the study of herbs throughout the U.S. to exchange ideas and keep in touch with her colleagues.

Dell Ratcliffe
Country Shepherd Herb News
Route 1, Box 107
Comer, GA 30629
Phone: 706-788-3116

Dell Ratcliffe has grown and used herbs for 18 years and is the editor and publisher of the *Country Shepherd Herb News,* a bimonthly herb newsletter for the Southeastern United States.

Terra Reneau
3597 Nottingham Court #3
Boulder, CO 80304
Phone: 303-541-9857

Terra Reneau is a practicing herbalist, medicine-maker and self-styled "sister to the plants." She left her home in Tennessee to come to Boulder, where she received certification as a clinical herbalist. She is currently working as a formulator at Nature's Apothecary Herbs and is a resident herbalist at the free herb clinic in Boulder. Terra's interests include gardening, working with Nature intelligences, astrology and all the many forms of healing and magical arts. She is an activist for our mother earth and all her many creatures.

Sara Klein Ridgley
3666 Marlesta Drive
San Diego, California 92111
Phone: 619-279-2670
Email: SaraKlein@aol.com

Sara Klein Ridgley has a Ph.D. in psychology and has studied homeopathy, herbal medicine, Ayurvedic medicine and nutrition since childhood. She is also a teacher of the Transcendental Meditation program. She lived in Israel until 1983 and currently lives and practices in San Diego, California

Andrea Rogers
Vineyard Vines
P.O. Box 774
Oak Bluffs, MA 02557
Phone: 508-693-8989
Fax: 508-693-1724

Andrea Rogers is a proprietor of Vineyard Vines, a home-based herbal business using organic herbs and flowers in freshly made skin care products that are sold at the Island Farmers Market on Martha's Vineyard during the summer.

She is also one of the founders of the Vineyard Artisans Festival, an annual event held each Labor Day weekend. This festival, made up of over 80 Island artisans who display their works to the public, is the biggest show on the Vineyard.

Jeanne Rose

219 Carl Street
San Francisco, CA 94117
Phone: 415-564-6785
Fax: 415-564-6799

Jeanne Rose, a California native daughter, is a leading pioneer in the revival of herbal and natural remedies and aromatherapy to maintain good health. She is also an international authority on the therapeutic uses of herbs, both medicinal and cosmetic, and a well-known teacher of aromatherapy since 1972.

In her lectures and teachings, Jeanne relates herbal applications to questions concerning health, hygiene, contraception, beauty and women's care as well as the environmental uses of plants, herbal animal care, herbal tradition and history, and the uses of essential oils to heal both the mind and the body. Her aromatic garden is world-famous and has appeared in *Herb Companion, Country Gardening* and the Japanese publication *Herb.*

The author of 12 herbal books plus a three-volume Herbal Studies Course and an Aromatherapy Course by correspondence, Jeanne has a rich background in plant use. Her latest book is *Herbs & Aromatherapy for the Reproductive System,* the first in a series of books addressing herbal and aromatic therapies for personal health. Her other books include: *Herbs & Things, The Herbal Body Book, Kitchen Cosmetics, Ask Jeanne Rose, The Herbal Guide to Food, The Modern Herbal* and *The Aromatherapy Book: Applications & Inhalations.*

Mary Ellen Ross

Merry Gardens
P.O. Box 595
Camden, ME 04843
Phone: 207-236-2121

Mary Ellen Ross started Merry Gardens Nursery on her own, more than 50 years ago. Although they initially did not encourage local trade, wanting to focus solely on mail order, Mary Ellen and her husband Ervin found they couldn't keep the public away. As a result, she created beautiful herb and perennial display gardens, along with lovely grounds and stands of wild flowers. Among Mary Ellen's many accomplishments is the founding of Merry Springs Park, a nature park straddling the Camden-Rockport line. She was instrumental in organizing the American Ivy Society and the International Geranium Society. She has continued to make education one of her primary goals, starting a junior garden club in 1970 with 10 children and offering horticultural classes on Saturday mornings. The TLC club, as it came to be known, earned a national award during its eight years of existence. Internationally recognized, the Rosses and Merry Gardens have appeared in magazine articles in *Yankee, Down East* and *National Geographic.* Mary Ellen has written many articles on plants and gardening, including a series for the *New York Times.*

Rachel Schneider
Flower Power Herbals
285 Webster Street
Newton, MA 02166
Phone: 617-964-8395

Rachel Schneider is a practicing herbalist and founder of Flower Power Herbals, a natural bodycare company combining herbs and the ancient art of aromatherapy. Rachel formulates a full line of original products from exotic massage oils to facial scrubs, balms, powders and more. Rachel is a member of the Northeast Herbal Association and the Association of Labor Assistants and Childbirth Educators.

Janice Schofield
Gardensong Herbs
Box 15213
Fritz Creek, Alaska 99603

Janice Schofield is passionate about plants. She was first lured into lifelong study by their tantalizing flavors. Her comprehensive herbal guide, *Discovering Wild Plants,* was a byproduct of seven years of research, interviews and field tests exploring edible and medicinal herbs while living in a remote Alaskan valley far beyond the end of the road. Plants have now dragged her back to town, business, (more) books and delving deeper into herbal healing. Janice is a 1995 graduate of the clinical herbalist program at New Mexico Herbal Center with herbalist/physician Tieraona Low Dog. She owns and operates Gardensong Herbs in Fritz Creek, Alaska, and teaches weekend and residential herbal classes. She is also the author of *Nettles, a Good Herb Guide* published by Keats Publishing, Inc.

Jan Shimp
Tyson, VT 05149
Phone: 802-228-4470

Jan Shimp has been practicing reflexology for ten years and Reiki for five years. She incorporates herbs, healing sounds and mudras into her healing work as well. She also trains horses, builds stone walls and is a ski instructor. Jan teaches classes on reflexology and alternative health for local businesses and community colleges. She is married, has two daughters, four horses and four dogs, all of whom benefit from her herbal and healing knowledge.

Vickie Shufer
4132 Blackwater Road
Virginia Beach, VA 23457
Phone: 804-421-3929
Email: wildfood@infi.net

For nearly 20 years, Vickie Shufer has been leading groups on field trips and conducting nature programs in public and private lands. She has led school groups, community groups and garden clubs and has worked as a teacher, tour guide and program coordinator for wildlife refuges and state parks in her area. She is the editor and publisher of *The Wild Foods Forum* newsletter, which is distributed nationwide. She has authored and illustrated two books: *A Coastal Ecology Coloring Book* and *A Naturalist's Field Guide to Coastal Communities.*

Karyn Siegel-Maier
5 Birchwood Drive South
Saugerties, NY 12477
Email: HerbalMuse@aol.com

Karyn Siegel-Maier is a free-lance journalist/columnist who specializes in herbs, alternative medicine and new age issues. Her publishing credits include national magazines such as *The Herb Quarterly* and *Healing Arts* (Canada); the newsletters, *Herban Lifestyles* and *Making Scents,* plus regional magazines and newspapers. Karyn is the author of six booklets pertaining to the medicinal and culinary use of herbs and herbal crafts published by the Herbal Muse Press. She is a contributing writer for the University of Washington's Online Medicinal Herb Library and author of *The Herbal Muse and Other Wise Things,* a self-syndicated column published in the Northeast for more than four years.

Rosemary Gladstar Slick
Box 420
E. Barre, VT 05649

"A long time ago when I was just a child," writes Rosemary Gladstar, "my grandmother took me to her gardens and introduced me to her weeds. She taught me how to knit with chicken feathers and showed me special games to play with bones she kept on her mantle. Her teachings were without fuss, strong and powerful like herself. That magic she taught me in the garden of my childhood has stayed with me throughout my life."

Rosemary Gladstar Slick is the founder of the California School of Herbal Studies, the Sage Mountain Botanical Sanctuary's Herbal Education Center and the past owner of Rosemary's Garden, an old-fashioned apothecary shop that has served Sonoma County for over a decade. Her experience includes 20 years in the herbal community as a healer, teacher, visionary and organizer of herbal events. She is also the founder of a new nonprofit organization called United Plant Savers, an organization dedicated to saving endangered and threatened medicinal plants. Rosemary lives on 500 acres of pristine Vermont wilderness.

Jane Smolnik
438 Will Dean Road
Springfield, VT 05156

Jane is an herbalist, nutritional consultant and owner of Crystal Garden Herbs. She has a 70-acre organic herb farm where she lives and works with her husband, a reflexologist, and her two home-schooled teenagers. They grow and harvest a wide variety of medicinal herbs in their many gardens, meadows and woodlands, as well as produce a full line of herbal extracts, teas and other remedies which they sell through their mail order catalog as well as to health food stores, co-ops and practitioners.

Jane teaches an herbal apprentice program, lectures and gives private consultations. She is a Cell Tech executive and shares blue-green algae with many people. Part Native American, she hosts monthly sweat lodge ceremonies with her native brothers and sisters.

7Song
Northeast School of Botanical Medicine
P.O. Box 6626
Ithaca, NY 14851
Phone: 607-564-1023

7Song, director of the Northeast School of Botanical Medicine, has been actively studying, teaching and pursuing his interest in plants for over 12 years. He graduated from the California School of Herbal Studies and the Southwest School of Botanical Medicine where he is currently on the faculty. He has taught throughout the U.S. at such places as the Ayurvedic Institute, Green Nations Gathering and The American Herbalist Guild. He has had a clinical practice for over four years, specializing in the unique health needs of men and long-term healthcare. After many years of working with people on acute and chronic health needs, he is continually inspired by the effectiveness of herbal therapies. He has made an extensive study of field botany and has traveled widely, gathering plants wherever he goes. 7Song has a deep and passionate love for plants and is working to bring herbal medicine back into current mainstream medical care.

Gail Ulrich
Blazing Star Herbal School
P.O. Box 6
Shelburne Falls, MA 01370
Phone: 413-625-6875

Gail Ulrich is founder and director of Blazing Star Herbal School in western Massachusetts and owner of New England Botanicals Herbal Products. An herbalist for over 20 years and a certified Flower Essence practitioner and instructor, Gail has organized the Annual Women's Herbal Conference in New England for the past nine years, and for the past three years, has joined Rosemary Gladstar Slick to create the largest gathering of its kind in New England. This conference is held in southern New Hampshire in August. Gail is also coorganizer (with Pam Montgomery and Kate Gilday) of the Annual Healing with Flowers Conference held in May each year.

She helped to formulate several national lines of herbal products, including a line of animal care products. She is a council member of the Northeast Herbal Association and a member of United Plant Savers. Gail lives on 26 acres of pine trees, rushing brooks, wildflower meadows and gardens in western Massachusetts with her astrologer husband, Don. Together, they have created an astrological garden, planted in the wheel of the zodiac, in accordance with the planetary rulers of each plant. Gail loves to work in her gardens, tell stories and concoct spicy dishes in her kitchen. She brings her love of herbs, wealth of personal experience and passion for teaching to all her work.

Joyce Wardwell
3936 Mount Bliss Road
East Jordan, MI 49727
Phone: 616-536-2877

Joyce Wardwell is an herbal teacher and educator, who teaches people how to incorporate wild plants into their daily lives for food, medicine, spirit and craft. She publishes *Herbal Voices,* a newsletter for a nationwide network of herbalists willing to share the insights they have learned working with plants. Members decide their own level of participation. Through

Herbal Voices, people contact each other to start/join herb groups or to exchange plants, seeds and research sources.

Joyce also leads workshops and seminars throughout the year to identify, gather, prepare and eat or use local plants. In addition to private medicinal herb consultations, she helps people learn to use the plants that grow on their own land, writes for several magazines and does hands-on herbal storytelling programs for grade schools.

Susun Weed
P.O. Box 64
Woodstock, NY 12498
Phone: 914-246-8081

"As a child," writes Susun Weed, "I went to sleep lullabied by the roars of lions and elephants. At the end of my block was an oak woods where I fell in love with nature. On the other side of that wild place was the Dallas Zoo. From these roots my fascination with plants, animals and all things wild has grown. Now I live on a homestead in the Catskills and my lullaby is the music of goats and cheese. I have an oak woods of my own and still love all that is wild. My life is devoted to helping women reclaim their wild nature, sharing with them the simple, safe remedies I know through teaching and writing."

Susun, a beloved author with four best-selling titles to her credit, is also an extraordinary teacher with a joyous spirit, a powerful presence and an encyclopedic knowledge of herbs and health. Her published titles include *Breast Cancer? Breast Health! The Wise Woman Way; Menopausal Years, The Wise Woman Way; Healing Wise;* and *Wise Woman Herbal for the Childbearing Year.* She teaches at her home base—the Wise Woman Center—her 55-acre homestead near Woodstock, N.Y., and throughout the United States, Canada, Australia, New Zealand, Holland and Germany. Susun has trained more than 150 apprentices and supervises nearly 200 correspondence course students. Susun is an initiated High Priestess of Dianic Wicca and a member of the Wolf Clan and the Sisterhood of the Shields.

Paula Wright
Sam'l Wells & Co.
Pondlick Herb Farm
7190 Pondlick Road
Seaman, OH 45679
Phone: 513-927-5283

Paula Wright is the current proprietor of Sam'l Wells & Co., which was once a fur and botanical trading post that first opened in 1826 on the banks of the Ohio River. There trappers and foragers would sell their merchandise of pelts and native roots, primarily the exotic ginseng. Today, it is the oldest ginseng company in the United States. It no longer deals in furs and has traded its Cincinnati roots for a new home on Pondlick Herb Farm, where the ginseng trade is now combined with Pondlick's cultivation and marketing of herbs and everlastings. In addition to serving as a brokerage firm for ginseng, the Wrights' company also wholesales goldenseal, culinary dried herbs and dried flowers such as statice, strawflowers and globe flowers, used for floral arrangements, perfumes and potpourri. All the flowers and culinary herbs are grown on the farm. There is also a retail shop filled with gifts crafted from everlasting flowers and herbs grown on the farm, as well as the work of local artisans. Pondlick Farm has also served as a cooperative farm for the study of the shiitake mushroom and there are plans to further research the cultivation practices of many medicinal herbs. "Most botanicals are still foraged for, which creates shortages for some herbs in the marketplace. Foraging also creates problems with extinction of some species such as wild ginseng," writes Paula, who wants to be involved in finding a solution for this problem. Classes and seminars are frequently offered at Pondlick on such subjects as "How to Forage for Wild Herbs." Paula also helps design and plant herb gardens.

Mary and Gregory Wulff-Tilford
Animals' Apawthecary
P.O. Box 212
Conner, MT 59827
Phone: 406-821-4090

Mary Wulff-Tilford, a professional herbalist and member of the American Herbalists Guild, devotes her time and expertise to the holistic care of animals. She has a certificate in natural therapies through the Australasian School of Herbal Studies, a certificate in phytotherapy through the National Institute of Medical Herbalists, and is studying veterinary homeopathy through the British Institute of Homeopathy to obtain a D.Hom. She is founder of Animals' Apawthecary, a company which produces low-alcohol herbal extracts for animals, is vice president of the Natural Pet Products Association, is on the board of the Lend-A-Paw Relief Organization as an herb advisor and is on the board of the Western Montana Spay and Neuter Task Force. Mary has coauthored articles on herbs for animals in *Natural Pet* magazine as well as a booklet called *Herbal Remedies for Dogs and Cats*. She and her husband, Greg, are currently completing a comprehensive, fully illustrated guidebook on herbs for animals, which is due to be published some time this year.

Gregory L. Tilford, coowner and formulating herbalist for Animals' Apawthecary, is a naturalist and herbalist who likes to cook and improvise his own recipes. He is a contributing editor and herb advisor for *Natural Pet* magazine and is the founding president of the Natural Pet Products Association. Greg is the author of two books on wild medicinal plants: *The Eco-Herbalists Fieldbook* and *Edible and Medicinal Plants of the West*. Greg and Mary live in the Rocky Mountains of western Montana, where they get their power from the sun, haul their water and grow their own food.

Jill Yeck
Peconic River Herb Farm
310-C River Road
Calverton, NY 11933

Herbalist Jill Yeck began as an apprentice at Peconic River Herb Farm in 1993 under the guidance of Cris Spindler, owner and leader of the farm.

When visitors arrive at Peconic River Herb Farm they are welcomed by a vinecovered arbor and a feeling of peace and beauty. Visitors are encouraged to meander through the many display gardens, visit the drying loft, explore the greenhouses where herbs, perennial plants and specialty plants are sold, examine the many herbal products and peruse the bookstore. Celebrating the seasons is one of the specialties at Peconic River Herb Farm. Delectable herbal recipes are always a part of these celebrations. Many special events at the farm highlight an herb of the season such as the Luxury of Lavender Day, Rose Tea and Tour, Garlic Festival and New World Chile Festival. Many kinds of culinary herbs and heirloom vegetables are grown at the farm and new recipes that use their many fresh herbs are always being invented. The Peconic River Herb Farm education program offers classes on many subjects such as how to start a garden, healthy cooking with herbs and herbal cosmetics.

RECOMMENDED READING

Here is a list of books and newsletters I trust and use often in my searches for herbal information:

HERBAL CRAFT AND HOW-TO BOOKS

The Complete Book of Flowers by Denise Diamond, Berkeley, CA, North Atlantic Books, 1990.
Herbs, How to Select, Grow and Enjoy by Norma Jean Lathrop, Tucson, AZ, HP Books, 1981.
HerbCraft: The Cultivation and Use of Herbs by Nerys Purchon and Dhenu Jennifer Clary, Australia, Hodder & Stoughton, 1990.

WILD FOOD GUIDES

Cattail Cakes and Chickweed Snakes, A Gourmet Wildfoods Cookbook by Debby Boots, Lake Elmore, VT, It's a Pleasure Publishing (P.O. Box 171, Lake Elmore, VT 05657), 1987. Wild food eating at its simplest and most fun!
Wild Foods Field Guide and Cookbook by Billy Joe Tatum, New York, Workman Publishing Company, 1976.

PLANT IDENTIFICATION BOOKS

Medicinal Plants, Peterson Field Guides by Steven Foster and James Duke, Boston, MA, Houghton Mifflin Company, 1990.
Newcomb's Wildflower Guide by Lawrence Newcomb, New York, Little, Brown and Company, 1977.

NEWSLETTERS AND BOOKS ABOUT HERBAL MEDICINE

The Village Healer, 15 South Hill Crossroads, Ludlow, VT 05149, 802-228-3967.
Herbal Voices, 3936 Mt. Bliss Rd., East Jordan, MI 49727, 616-536-2877.
Joe Pye & Friends Herbal Network Newsletter, Capital Area Herbal Network, P.O. Box 5022, Springfield, VA 22150-5022.
American Herb Association Quarterly Newsletter, P.O. Box 173, Nevada City, CA 95959
Northeast Herbal Association Newsletter, P.O. Box 479, Milton, NY 12547.
Medical Herbalism—A Clinical Newsletter for the Herbal Practitioner, P.O. Box 33080, Portland, OR 97233.
A Male Herbal by James Green, Freedom, CA, Crossing Press, 1991.
A Modern Herbal by Maude Grieve, NY, Dover Publications, two volumes, 1971.
The Roots of Healing: A Woman's Book of Herbs by Deb Soule, NY, Carol Publishing Group, 1995.
The Holistic Herbal by David Hoffmann, Dorset, England, Element Books, 1983.
Health, Happiness and the Pursuit of Herbs by Adele G. Dawson, Lexington, MA, Stephen Greene Press, 1980.
Healing Wise by Susun Weed, Woodstock, NY, Ash Tree Publishing, 1989.
Sage Healing Ways Booklets (*Natural Cosmetics, Herbs for Children, Herbs for the Nervous System, Herbal Medicinal Preparations, Herbs for Women's Health, Herbs for Winter Health, Herbs for the Liver,* and *Rosemary's Wildfood Recipes*) by Rosemary Gladstar Slick, Barre, VT, Sage Publications.

INDEX

After-Baby Tea, 44
Albano, Jo-Ann, 26, 48, 109, 211
Albert, Susan Wittig, 17, 28, 57, 133, 176, 177, 211–212
alfalfa, 35, 36, 37, 45, 125, 206
Alfs, Matthew, 40, 212
allergies, edible flowers, 18
Allyn, Sheryl, 10, 162, 163, 212
amaranth, 47, 206
  substitutes for, 82
Andrews-Miller, Sharleen, 23, 43, 44, 71, 72, 90, 146, 189, 213
angelica leaves, 93, 206
Anise Dessert Bars, 182
anise hyssop flowers, 182
Anti-Inflammatory Tea, 41
Aphrodisiac Honey, 180
appetizers, 9–13, 169
Aromatherapy, A Complete Guide to the Healing Art, 224
arrowroot, 67
Ask Jeanne Rose, 241
astragalus root, 31, 206
Aunt Althea's Homepun Homilies, 217
avocado, 10, 137

Baked Garlic, 11
Ballis, Maia, 28, 53, 54, 73, 100, 122, 213
Banana No-Cream Pie, 186
bark, medicinal use of, 31, 206
Barley sugar, 182

Barley Vegetable Soup, 85
basil, 7, 9, 19, 24, 46, 64, 68, 69, 73, 85, 92, 97, 103, 118, 127, 198, 206
  medicinal use of, 198
Basil Walnut Dressing, 73
bay leaf, 83, 93, 116
beans, 83, 93
Bee Pollen Energy Balls, 22
bee pollen granules, 22
beef, 148, 164
Bennet, Robin Rose, 58, 139, 160, 180, 214
Better Butter, 117
beverages, 24–45
Bigfoot, Peter, 104, 105, 214
biscuits, 105–106
  cutting, 106
bitters, medicinal use, 120
black birch, 77
black haw root, 41, 206
Black Walnut Honey Butter, 115
black walnuts (*Juglans nigra*)
  medicinal use of, 115
Blue, Sage, 41, 215
borage, 9, 42, 206
Bove, Mary, 27, 78, 101, 154, 215
breakfast dishes, 197-203
Breast Cancer? Breast Health!, 124, 247
broccoli, 14, 156
brown rice, 7, 20, 134, 141, 154
Brown, Carole, 19, 45, 216

Brussels sprouts, 14
burdock *(Articum lappa)*, 21, 33, 39,
    41, 58, 80, 140, 141, 142
  blooms, 159
  medicinal use of, 143, 206
  stems, 139
Burdock Bloom Spike Bake, 159
Burdock Kimpira, 142
Burdock Vinegar, 58
Burdock with Miso and Lemon Peel,
    140
Buttermilk and Herb Ice Cream, 196
butters, 115–118

cabbage (*brassica*), 124, 125
  medicinal use, 14
Cafe'de Olla, 26
Calcium Tea, 45
calendula(*Calendula officinalis*)
  medicinal use of, 8, 206
  petals, 106
Calendula, 224
Candied Angelica, 182
Calendula Biscuits, 106
Caraway Cake, 194
caraway seed, 53, 194
cardamom, 26, 194, 206
Carden, Jane, 89, 101, 103, 157, 184,
    193, 216
Cardoons, 139
carnations, 9
Carrot Chive Soup, 91
Carrots with Cumin and Ginger, 123
carrots, 91, 123, 128, 142, 144, 145
catnip, 45, 206
cauliflower, 14, 19, 144
Cayenne Jump Start, 25
cayenne peppers, 64, 65, 83, 206
Celebration Tea, 37
celery, 99
celery seed, 53, 206

chamomile, 27, 36, 42, 43, 44, 45, 206
Change of Season Brew, 39
  cheese, 15, 107, 150, 172, 174, 184,
    199
  cottage cheese, 110
  mozzarella, 110–111
  parmesan, 103, 109, 110–111, 127
chervil, 72
Chi Balls, 22
Chichon, Pat, 139, 216–217
chicken, 16, 17, 89, 161, 162
Chicken and Noodle Soup, 89
Chicken mushroom (*Polyporus sul-
    phureus*), 170
Chicken salad, 17
Chicken with Thyme and Red Onion
    Vinaigrette, 16
chickpeas, 58, 139
Chickpeas and Roses, 139
chickweed, 7, 58, 59, 206
chicory root, 39, 206
chiles, 69
Chili-Basil Sauce, 97
Chilled Sage Blossom and Cucumber
    Soup, 78
Chilled Vegetable medley, 128
China's Garden, 211
chives, 15, 20, 24, 49, 65, 68, 73, 86,
    91, 107, 108
Chocolate Coffee, 26
Chocolate Tea, 26
chutney, 96, 134
cicely leaves, 93
cilantro (*Coriandrum sativum*), 67,
    177
cinnamon, 26, 38, 43, 44, 179, 194,
    206
Clover Noodles, 152
cloves, 26, 46, 64
Coconut Ice Cream, 196
"Coffee," 25

Cohen, Russ, 115, 159, 174, 181, 217
"Cold Kicker" Crystal-Infused Medicinal Herbal Vinegar, 64
collards, 14
comfrey leaf, 45
Complete Herbal Handbook for Farm and Stable, 230
Complete Herbal Handbook for the Dog and Cat, 230
cookies, 176, 178, 180, 181
coriander (*Coriandrum sativum*), 17, 51, 52
    medicinal use of, 177, 206
Coriander Crisps, 177
Cottage Herb Bread, 110
Country Shepherd Herb News, 86, 87, 239
Creamy Squash Soup, 90
Crone Candy, 22
cronewort, 89, 206
Cronewort Vinegar, 89
Crystallization, decorative, 183
cumin, 17, 85, 206
Curried Chicken-of-the-Woods, 134
Curried Wild Greens, 131
Curried Wild Rice with Lentils, 134
curry, 54, 81, 122, 131–134

Daily Flax Shake, 203
damiana, 38, 206
dandelion
    greens, 24, 47, 58, 76,110–111, 118, 119, 125, 126, 138, 199, 203
        cooking of, 166
    petals, 200
    roots, 13, 25, 33, 34, 39, 63, 80, 149
        medicinal uses of, 34, 206
Dandelion Balsamic Vinegar, 63
Dandelion Breakfast Smoothie, 203
Dandelion Dip, 51
Dandelion Gravy, 126

Dandelion Green Soup, 76
Dandelion Italiano, 119
Dandelion Matzo Ball Soup, 92
Dandelion Pancakes, 200
Dandelion Pizza Sandwich, 137
Dandy Burgers, 138
Dandy Rhubarb Crisps, 191
decoctions, description of, 33
Delightfully Delicious Daylily, 221
desserts, 176–196
"Devil Made Me Do It" eggs, 9
dill, 7, 9, 53, 73, 91, 107, 108, 206
Dill and Potato Cakes, 107
dips and spreads, 46–57, 137
Discovering Wild Plants, 242
Dixon, Althea, 153, 217
Dreier, Ruth, 122, 141, 142, 218
dressings, 66–74
dried herbs, buying, 38
dried to fresh herbs ratio, 2, 93
Druid Herbal for the Sacred Earth Year, 226
D'Terra, Donna, 140, 142, 218
Duffy, Kathleen, 25, 27, 35, 81, 219
Dunning, Judy, 35, 64, 69, 151, 219–220
Dwinell, Jane, 85, 91, 92, 220

Easy Homemade Mustard, 57
echinacea angustifolia root, 31, 206
Echinacea/Sheep Sorrel Dressing, 70
eggplant, 122, 150
Eggplant & Mustard, 122
Eggplant Lasagna, 150
elder, 231
elderberries, 201
    medicinal use of, 185, 206
Elderberry Tart, 185
Elder Blossom Pudding, 190
elder flower, medicinal use, 190, 206
elk, marinade for, 163

Epicurean Delights No-salt Herb & Spice Blend, 128
Epicurean Delights Lemon Pepper, 162
Epicurean Delights Mediterranean Herb Blend, 165

Fairy Food Casserole, 155
Far Eastern Vegetable Bake, 157
Favorite Fast Cabbage, 124
Feelgood Tea, 36
fennel, 7, 32, 36, 86, 100, 110–111, 151, 192
   medicinal use of, 100, 206
Fennel and Ginger Wine, 32
Fennel Cake with Lavender Frosting, 192
Fennel Lime Sauce, 100
fenugreek
   medicinal use of, 52, 206
   seeds, 51
   sprouts, 20
15-Minute Herbal Fish, 159
Finneyfrock, Tina, 26, 39, 135, 181, 220–221
fireweed, 40
fish, 159, 168
Flax Bread, 114
Flax For Cereal, 202
Flax Pancakes, 201
flaxseed, 84, 114, 201, 202, 203, 206
   egg and oil substitute, 195
   medicinal use of, 202
   toppings, 141
Flower Fritters, 138
flowers, edible, 18
"For the Blues Tea," 42
French sorrel, 19
Fresh Elderberry Syrup, 201
Fresh Tomato Basil Soup, 92
Fruit Fix, 183

Gail, Peter, 92, 111, 126, 137, 138, 191, 199, 203, 221
Gardiner, Colette, 63, 171, 222
garlic, 65, 67, 68, 86, 87, 94, 95, 116, 120, 206
Garlic and Herb Vinegar, 65
Garlic Butter, 116
Garlic Soup, 86
Geller, Cascade Anderson, 11, 49, 222
German Cabbage, 125
Gileadi-Sweet, Cathy, 84, 114, 141, 201, 202, 203, 222–223
ginger, 10, 13, 21, 25, 32, 36, 43, 69, 76, 89, 95, 99, 123, 125, 173, 179, 194
   medicinal use of, 95, 206
Ginger Crisps, 179
Ginger Dandelion Buds, 125
Ginger-Garlic Sesame Sauce, 95
Gobo: see burdock roots, 143
gomashio, 53, 54, 122, 142
"Good medicine" salad, 7
Grandma Mornis' 3-Herb Bread, 108
Graves, Judith, 9, 14, 15, 29, 127, 144, 164, 187, 189, 223
Great Dandelion Cookbook, 92, 111, 126, 137, 138, 191, 221
Green Corn Bread, 104
green flours, making of, 153
Green Herb Dressing, 73
Green, James, 120
Green Mansion salad, 14
Green, Mindy, 201, 224
Green Rice Salad, 20
greens, 18, 20, 21, 24, 47, 59, 131, 172, 173, 174
   substitutes for, 82
guacamole, 137
Gypsy Fever, formula, 185, 190

Happy House Tea, 43
hawthorne leaves, 41
Healing Magic: Wisdom of the Moon, Women, and Plants, 214
Heartiest Cake, 194
Heart's Delight Herbs, 169
Herb & Spice Gazette, 230
Herb and Garlic Salt, 68
Herb and Vegetable Stir-Fry, 144
Herb Butter, 118
Herb Companion, 212
herb ratios, 2, 93
Herb Roasted Nuts, 23
Herbal Body Book, 241
Herbal Earth Newsletter, 233
herbal flowers, edible, 18
Herbal Guide to Food, 241
Herbal Punch, 27
Herbal Remedies for Dogs and Cats, 249
"Herbal Serendipity," 181
herbalist profiles, 2, 211–250
Herbed Chicken, 162
Herbed Rice, 135
herbs
    crushing of, 91
    drying of, 5
    food use, 1, 2, 93, 98
    harvesting times, 3–4, 17, 50, 132
Herbs & Aromatherapy for the Reproductive System, 241
Herbs & Things, 241
Herbs for Healthy Skin, Hair and Nails, 231
Hertzler, Melissa, 147, 148, 224–225
hibiscus, 35, 37, 38
Hilba, 51
Holmes, Caroline, 60, 182, 183, 225
Hopman, Ellen Evert, 31, 170, 226
hops, 38, 206

Horn of Plenty mushroom (*Craterellus cornucopioides*), 170
horseradish, 25, 206
Hot and Spicy Vinegar, 65
Hot Chile Vinegar, 64
Hot Honey Mustard, 56
Hummus sandwich, 58

Immune-Boosting Roots and Herb Potage, 80
Impossible Custard Pie, 187
infusions, description of, 33
Italian Herb Bread, 109

jalapeno peppers, 94, 104
jam and jelly, 60–61
Jenner, Jo, 83, 84, 185, 186, 226
Jones, Feather, 6, 9, 30, 51, 93, 107, 113, 125, 227
Joy Balls, 22
Joy's Mushroom Sage Sauce, 98
Judi's Dandylion Pizza Bread, 110–111

Kahn, Michael Jonas, 19, 73, 150, 154, 227–228
kale, 14
Kashi and Broccoli Casserole, 156
Keith, Bryan Ray, 66, 68, 70, 80, 83, 228
kelp, 10, 11, 68, 80
King, Penny, 178, 196, 228–229
Kitchen Cosmetics, 241
kohlrabi, cabbage family, 14
Kress, Henrietta, 126, 229

lamb's quarter, nutritional value, 132, 206
Lamb's Quarter Salad, 6
lavender, 43, 44, 45, 192, 206
    blossoms, buying, 176

Lavender Shortbread Cookies, 176
Lawrenson, Michelle, 38, 161, 229
Lawrenson, Tom, 38, 161, 229
Lawry's Seasoned Salt, 19
leadplant, 40
Lemon-Aid Tea, 35
Lemon and Herb Marinade, 165
lemon balm (*Melissa officinalis*), 14,
    27, 28, 39, 43, 44, 45, 125, 144, 159
  medicinal use of, 145, 206
lemon grass, 35, 36, 89
lemon thyme, 7, 55
Lemon Thyme Ice Cubes, 27
Lemon Thyme Mustard, 55
lemon verbena, 35, 36, 117, 159, 184,
    186
Lemon Verbena Bread, 195
Lentil Loaf, 154
lentils, 83, 134, 154
Letson, Allie, 128, 162, 164, 165,
    230
Levy, Juliette de Bairacli, 29, 52, 118,
    129, 190, 196, 230
licorice root, 35, 38, 41, 45, 206
Look! The Wild Swans, 230
lovage, 14, 49, 107, 164, 206
Low-fat Garlic and Herb Salad Dress-
    ing, 67

mace, 71
main dishes, 130–174; see also cur-
    ries
Make-Ahead Sausage and Dandelion
    Breakfast, 199
Male Herbal, The, 120
mallow, 125
  medicinal use of, 104, 206
Mama's Meat Balls, 164
Manchester, Julie, 42, 117, 158, 195,
    231
Maple Mustard, 57

marigold (*Calendula officinalis*),
    medicinal use of, 8
marinades, 160, 163, 165
marjoram, 10, 19, 68, 72, 90, 206
Mars, Brigitte, 81, 197, 231
*Marvelous Mustards and Curious
    Curries*, 57, 133
Mashed Potatoes with Nettles, 126
McCampbell, Harvest, 65, 67, 68,
    116, 232
McKenna, Christine, 55, 232
meadowsweet, 41, 206
Meal in a Bundle, 164
Meatballs, 148
Mediterranean Pork Chops, 165
*Menopausal Years, The Wise Woman
    Way*, 88, 183, 247
Mexican Spice Soup, 85
Midnight Madness Tea, 38
milk thistle
  medicinal use of, 66, 206
  seeds, 66
mint, 72, 96
  medicinal uses of, 28, 206
Mint and Pea Salad, 15
miso paste, 53, 76, 80, 85, 88, 140
Mock Potato Salad, 19
Modern Herbal, The, 241
Morning Biscuits with Rosemary,
    105
Mornis, Risa, 46, 58, 74, 98, 108, 117,
    152, 186, 198, 200, 233
Motherhood Tea: see After-Baby Tea
mugwort (*Artemisia vulgaris*), 89
mullein, 40, 45, 206
Murphy, Sharon, 137, 156, 234
Murray, Andrea, 76, 97, 121, 192, 234
Mushroom Burger, 137
mushrooms, 10, 11, 88, 98, 134, 136,
    145, 149, 155, 167
  harvesting wild, 12

shiitake, 80, 85
types of wild, 170
mustard greens, cabbage family, 14
mustard seed, 14, 21, 55, 56, 57,
206

Nagler, Suzanne, 13, 80, 149, 235
Nana Theresa's Spaghetti Sauce, 147
Nardozzi, Barbara, 47, 235
nasturtium, 9
blossoms,17
Nature's Children, 29, 52, 129
Navy Bean and Vegetable Soup, 93
Nesto (Nettle Pesto), 48
Nettle Dumplings, 84
Nettle Lasagne, 149
Nettle Lentil Soup, 83
Nettle Loaf, 154
Nettle Pie, 171
Nettle Salad Dressing, 74
Nettle Vinegar, 74
nettles (*Urtica species*), 19, 39, 44, 48,
80, 83, 122, 125, 136, 149, 154,
197, 206, 243
nutritional value of, 50
Nettles, 243
Nettles Florentine, 197
Nettles-Tempeh Melt, 136
Non-Vinegar Herbal Salad Dressing,
72
noodles, making, 153

oat straw, 38, 43, 44
Olive Basil Muffins with Parmesan
Topping, 103
O'Mara, Kathleen, 166, 236
Onions & Thyme, 129
orange peel, 35, 43, 44
oregano, 65, 68, 93, 103, 118, 206
Oyster mushroom (*Pleurotus ostrea-
tus*), 170

Page, Kiyra, 15, 67, 145, 236–237
Palmer, Mary Pat, 39, 194, 237
pansies, 9, 59
Pansy Punch, 29
paprika, 19, 23, 53, 71, 73, 99, 159
parsley, 46, 53, 70, 73, 78, 83, 85, 86,
90, 108, 110, 123, 206
part, measurement, 37
pasta, 151, 152
Pastor, Bonnie, 35, 64, 69, 151,
219–220
Pastry Crust, 187
peanuts, 146
Peconic River Herb Farm Lemon
Verbena Peaches, 184
*People of the Earth—The New Pagans
Speak Out*, 226
peppercorns, 64
peppermint, 36, 37, 42, 44
peppers (hot), 94, 97, 101
pesto, 46
freezing of, 48
Pesto Pasta, 152
Pickeled Dandelion Roots, 13
Pickeled Ginger, 13
pie crusts, 186, 187
Pineapple Garden Punch, 28
plantain,47
Poitras, Sonia, 65, 238
poppy seeds, 10, 71
portabello mushrooms, 145
Portabello Romanoff, 145
potatoes, 120, 126
Potato Salad, 19
pot marigold: see calendula
Puri, H. S., 96, 238

Queen Anne's Lace (*Daucus carota*),
77
medicinal use of, 61, 206
Queen Anne's Lace Jelly, 61

Quick Quiche, 166
Quintana, Linda, 110, 188, 239

Raspberry-Lemon Verbena Butter, 117
Raspberry Vinegar, 72
Ratcliffe, Dell, 86, 87, 239
red clover, 27, 35, 36, 206
red raspberry leaf, 44, 45, 206
Reneau, Terra, 22, 155, 239–240
rhubarb, 99, 188, 189, 191
Rhubarb and Ginger Remoulade, 99
Rhubarb Bread Pudding, 189
Rhubarb Pie with Cicely, 188
rice, 10 131, 134, 135, 144, 155, 156; see also brown rice
Ridgley, Sara Klein, 20, 51, 52, 240
Roasted Garlic and Red Chile Pepper Purée, 94
Roasted Garlic Potatoes, 120
Roasted Sesame Milk Thistle Salad Dressing Mix, 66
Rodgers, Andrea, 159, 240
roots, used in soup, 80
rose hips, 36, 37, 42, 43, 60, 178
  medicinal use of, 101, 206
Rosehip and Apple jam, 60
Rose Hip Cookies, 178
Rose Hip Honey, 178
Rose Hip Sauce, 101
Rose, Jeanne, 169, 178, 241
rosemary, 10, 36, 90, 101, 105, 109, 110–111, 120, 206
Rosemary Spiced Pear Sauce, 101
roses, 139, 206
Ross, Mary Ellen, 90, 175, 241–242
Ruth's Burdock and Brown Rice Dinner, 141

Sacred Smoke, 232
SAD Tonic, 39

saffron, substitute for, 8
Saffron-Currant Refrigerator Cookies, 180
Sage Mountain Wild Foods, 131
sage, 78, 86, 90, 98, 109, 206
salads, 6–10, 13–20
salt, substitutes for, 81, 158
salves, marigold, 8
sandwiches, 57-59
sassafras root, 21, 41, 77
sauces, 94–102
savory, 68
Scarborough Fair Seasoning, 90
Schneider, Rachel, 13, 64, 78, 125, 167, 182, 242
Schofield, Janice, 10, 24, 48, 242–243
Sea Vegeta-Balls, 121
seaweeds, 7, 10, 11, 47, 68, 85, 88, 121, 124, 141, 173
  nutritional value, 11
seeds
  drying of, 5
  measurement of, 2
Sensual-A-Tea, 35
sesame salt (gomashio), 53, 54, 142
sesame seeds, 7, 10, 52, 66, 140
7Song, 33, 245
Shar's Raspberry Poppy Seed Vinaigrette, 71
sheep sorrel (*Rumex acetosella*), 47, 59, 70
  medicinal use of, 79
shiitake mushrooms,134, 136, 149
  medicinal use of, 135
Shimp, Jan, 107, 195, 243
Shufer, Vickie, 59, 138, 172, 243
Siberian ginseng, 22, 31, 45, 206
Siegal-Maier, Karyn, 105, 106, 179, 180, 194, 244
skullcap, 42, 45, 206
Slick, Rosemary Gladstar, 131, 244

smartweed, 77
Smoked Salmon-Nettle Fritatta, 168
Smolnik, Jane, 85, 134, 173, 245
snacks, 21–23
solomon's seal roots, 21
sorrel, 24, 77, 78
Sorrel Soup, 78
soups, 75–94
   flax dumplings, 84
Southwest Angel Hair & Wild Fennel, 151
spearmint, 15, 27, 35, 43, 44
spiceberries, 21
spicebush, 77
Spiced Tofu (Mock Egg Salad), 53
Spicy Apple Cake, 193
Spicy Kelp Rings, 10
Spicy Peanut Noodle Salad, 146
Spinach and Feta Salad, 15
Spinach or Stinging Nettle Dip, 49
spinach, 15, 166
spirulina, 22
Spring Delight Sandwich, 58
Spring Greens with Sherry Vinaigrette, 18
Spring Herb Dip, 49
squash, 90, 127, 128
Steamed Nettles, 122
stevia, 42, 45, 53, 73, 194
Stimul-A-Tea, 36
Stong Bone Stew, 88
Strawberry-Apple-Spearmint Juice, 28
Strawberry Lemon Cold Elixir, 31
Strawberry Syrup, 29
Stuffed Mushrooms, 169
Sun-Dried Tomato Vinaigrette, 69
sunflower seeds, 122, 124, 194
Sun Mountain Natural Foods Cookbook, 28, 53, 54, 73, 100, 122, 213
Sunshine Quiche, 167

sun tubers, 21
Sushi Salad, 10
Sweet Basil Tofu Omelette, 198
Sweet cicely (*Myrrhis odorata*), 188, 206
sweetfern, 77
sweetgale, 21, 77
Sweet Lavender Oranges, 184
Sweet Wild Pickles, 21
Swiss Cheese Loaf, 107

tarragon, 7, 49, 56, 64, 67, 68, 72, 73, 206
Tarragon Mustard, 56
Tarragon Mustard Salad Dressing, 67
Taylor's Tarragon Wafers, 175
Three Seaweed Dressing, 68
Thumbprint Cookies, 181
thyme, 16, 19, 52, 68, 72, 83, 86, 90, 109, 122, 129
   medicinal use of, 17, 206
Thyme and Seasons Herbal Teas, 17, 28, 176, 177
Thyme Tea, 17
tofu, 53, 54, 58, 186, 198
Tofu Curry, 54
Tofu "Egg" salad sandwich, 58
Tom's World-Famous Chicken Recipe, 161
Tomato, Basil and Red Onion Salad, 9
Tomato Herb Salad, 7
Totally Free Lunch, The, 221
Traveler's Joy, 230
Tree Medicine, Tree Magic, 226
turmeric, 53, 57, 206

udon noodles, 146
Ulrich, Gail, 95, 134, 136, 246

Vanilla-scented Sugar, 189
vegetables, 119–129, 157

venison, marinade for, 163
vinegars, 58, 62–65, 72, 74, 89
    basic preparation, 62–63
violets, 59, 206
    medicinal purposes of, 60
V-6 Juice, 24
Vitali-Tea: see After-Baby Tea
vitex berries, 41, 206

Wardwell, Joyce, 12, 21, 25, 32, 77, 99, 102, 246–247
Warming Winter Tea, 33
wasabi horseradish, 10
Weed, Susun, 88, 119, 124, 183, 247
Whole Wheat No-butter Crust, 186
Wholistic Healing for the Family, 220
Wild Berry Sauce, 102
wild carrot, 61; see also Queen Anne's Lace
wildcrafted herbal teas, 40
wildcrafting, 3–4
Wild Crockpot Stew, 163
Wild Eggrolls, 173
Wildflower Pitas, 59
Wildflowers, gathering of, 59
Wild Foods Forum, The, 212, 243
wild ginger, 77, 206
Wild Green Burritos, 172

Wild Greens Pesto, 47
Wild Greens Spanikopita, 174
wild greens, substitutes for, 82
wild leeks, 77
Wild Mushroom Caviar, 12
Wild Rose-Ade, 30
wild seasonings, 77
Wild Thing Soup, 81
wild yam root, 41, 206
Wise Woman Herbal for the Child-bearing Years, 119, 247
Wise Woman Healing Ways, 160
wood betony, 45, 206
wood sorrel, 59
Wright, Paula, 16, 18, 69, 248
Wulff-Tilford, Gregory, 72, 163, 249
Wulff-Tilford, Mary, 72, 249

yarrow, 77, 206
Yeck, Jill, 49, 94, 120, 184, 249–250
yellow dock (*Rumex crispus*), 39, 113
    medicinal use of, 112, 206
Yellow Dock Seed Bread, 113
yellow sweet clover, 77

Za'arta, 52
Zoom balls, 22
zucchini, 127, 145
Zucchini Rounds, 127